ALLERGIES

—Diseases and People—

ALLERGIES

Sara L. Latta

Enslow Publishers, Inc.

44 Fadem Road	PO Box 38
Box 699	Aldershot
Springfield, NJ 07081	Hants GU12 6BP
USA	UK

Library of Congress Cataloging-in-Publication Data

Latta, Sara L.
    Allergies / Sara L. Latta
        p. cm. — (Diseases and people)
    Includes bibliographical references and index.
    Summary: Explores the history of information about allergies and discusses
symptoms, diagnosis, prevention, and treatments.
    ISBN 0-7660-1048-1
    1. Allergy—Juvenile literature. [1. Allergy.] I. Title. II. Series.
RC585.L37   1998
616.97—dc21   97-34156
                                       CIP
                                       AC

Printed in the United States of America

10 9 8 7 6 5 4 3 2

Illustration Credits: Al Bello, Allsport Photography (USA) Inc., p. 11; ALK
Laboratories, Inc., p. 40; A.M. Dvorak, et al., International Archives of Allergy and
Immunology 1996, p. 92; AOCS Press, p. 69; Becky Mead, pp. 29, 31, 33; Center
Laboratories, p. 81; © Corel Corporation, pp. 45, 52, 86; *FDA Consumer*, p. 63;
National Library of Medicine, p. 16; M. Williams, University of Illinois, p. 23; Sara
Latta, pp. 28, 58, 65, 75.

Cover Illustration: © Corel Corporation and AOCS Press (bottom right).

Contents

Acknowledgments

The author thanks Sheldon Cohen, scientific advisor and National Institute of Allergy and Infectious Disease scholar at the National Library of Medicine, and John C. Brown, professor of microbiology at the University of Kansas, for their careful reading of portions of the manuscript and their many helpful comments and suggestions. The author also thanks John A. Fling, M.D., associate professor at the University of North Texas, Health Science Center at Fort Worth, and Jack E. Fincham, Ph.D., dean of the School of Pharmacy, University of Kansas, for their time in reviewing the manuscript and their helpful suggestions.

ALLERGIES

What are allergies? Allergies are the result of an abnormally sensitive immune response to a foreign substance, called an allergen.

Who gets allergies? Anyone can develop allergies. An estimated 20 percent of the American population has allergies.

How do you get allergies? Allergic reactions occur when a sensitive person breathes, touches, eats, or drinks an allergen. The tendency to develop allergies may be inherited or provoked.

What are the symptoms? Symptoms vary, depending on the site where the allergic reaction occurs, although itching, swelling, and redness are all common. Allergic reactions in the respiratory system often result in sneezing, excess mucus production, and, in the case of allergic asthma, difficult breathing.

How are allergies treated? Allergies can often be treated with a variety of drugs that reduce allergic symptoms and inflammation of the involved tissues. Some allergies respond well to allergy shots (immunotherapy), which modify the immune response to allergens.

How can allergies be prevented? For those who are allergy-prone, avoiding the allergen is currently the best form of prevention.

1

Allergies: They Are Nothing to Sneeze At

Swimmer Amy Van Dyken won four gold medals at the 1996 Olympic Games in Atlanta—the first United States woman ever to win four golds in a single Olympics. Watching the twenty-three-year-old sprinter slice through the water like a shark chasing its prey, it is hard to believe she was once considered a "little asthmatic weakling" who could not swim the length of a pool until she was twelve years old.[1] Her severe asthma attacks often sent her to the emergency room of the hospital, fighting for every breath. Amy's asthma attacks—like those of most young people with asthma—were usually triggered by allergies.

Allergies are caused by immune system reactions. The immune system is a collection of cells and molecules that recognize and destroy harmful invaders such as viruses or bacteria. For most people, most of the time, the immune system works splendidly. We could not survive without our immune systems. In some people, however, the immune system is an overachiever, launching a similar attack on normally harmless substances called allergens. The allergic reaction, as the attack is called, gets rid of the allergens. But in the process it also damages some of the body's cells, producing the symptoms we associate with allergies. Sometimes the damage is permanent.

In Amy's case, allergic reactions caused the airways in her lungs to tighten up, making it hard for her to breathe. The mucus-producing cells in her airways worked overtime, further decreasing airflow. Amy's allergens seemed to be everywhere. Her mother had to remove the stuffed animals from her room—they attracted dust. She covered the air vents with damp cheesecloth. And she vacuumed the floor again and again. "I lived with so much guilt," Amy's mother said. "She would have an attack, and I would wonder if it was because I hadn't vacuumed enough. But it is impossible to keep a home 100 percent dust-free."[2] Amy could not go to the zoo—she was allergic to the animals. She could not do gymnastics—she was allergic to the chalk dust.

When Amy was six, one of her doctors suggested that she might try swimming indoors—the warm, humid air often blocks asthma attacks. Amy had to work hard to build up her stamina, but she kept at it, and won her first race at the age of thirteen. Today, Amy still has allergies and asthma, but she keeps them under control—most of the time—by avoiding the allergens that trigger her attacks and by taking her medication.[3]

Amy Van Dyken rejoices after the 50-meter freestyle final at the Olympics in Atlanta, 1996.

Allergies Are Common

Amy has a lot of company. About one in five Americans is allergic to something. Allergic rhinitis, often called hay fever, is the most common allergic disease, affecting perhaps 15 percent of all Americans.[4] It is an allergic reaction in the nose and throat to airborne particles like pollen (the spores grown on plants), microscopic dust mites, or animal dander (skin flakes).

If the allergic reaction to airborne particles occurs in the airways of the lungs instead, it can cause asthma, the most common chronic illness in childhood. In the United States, asthma affects an estimated 14 to 15 million people, including 4.8 million under the age of eighteen. Unfortunately, asthma-related hospitalizations and deaths are on the rise, especially among young African Americans.[5]

Some people are allergic to certain foods. Food allergies are common in childhood. As many as 10 percent of infants and children develop allergies to one or more foods, but they often outgrow these allergies as they reach adulthood.[6] Other common allergens include certain drugs (for example, penicillin, aspirin, and codeine), food additives (such as sulfites), insect venom, poison ivy, nickel, some makeup ingredients, and latex.

The symptoms of allergies can vary, depending on the allergen and the location of the allergic reaction. For some people, allergies mean sniffling and sneezing. Others, especially those with asthma, wheeze and gasp for breath. Some allergens can cause hives (small, itchy white bumps surrounded by red inflamed areas on the skin) or skin rashes. Occasionally—especially in response to penicillin, insect stings, or peanuts—the allergic reaction may take the form of anaphylaxis. This is a serious allergic reaction that takes place throughout the body. Sometimes the throat and breathing passages swell, making it difficult or impossible to breathe. Anaphylaxis can cause a sudden drop in blood pressure, shock, and even death.

Various over-the-counter and prescription drugs are available to treat allergy symptoms, from the occasional seasonal sniffle and sneeze to the asthmatic's wheeze. Allergy shots can make life less miserable for some people. For those unlucky few who experience anaphylaxis, emergency measures can be lifesavers. The best way to prevent allergic reactions is to recognize and avoid the allergens that cause them.

Most of the allergy drugs available treat the symptoms, but not the cause of the disease. That could soon change. A number of researchers are studying ways to halt allergic reactions before they start. "We are no longer going to just treat asthma and allergic rhinitis," says Dr. John Selner, director of the Allergy Respiratory Institute in Denver. "We're going to technologically alter those diseases."[7] Scientists are also hot on the trail of the genes that cause some people to develop allergies. They hope that a better understanding of the genetic causes of the disease will allow them to develop better allergy drugs, or perhaps even prevent allergies from emerging altogether.

2

How We Came to Understand Allergies

Accounts of allergic reactions are nearly as old as the written record itself. Hieroglyphics on the tomb of King Menes of Egypt, dating from around 2600 B.C., show that he died from an allergic reaction to an insect sting, probably a wasp or hornet. Descriptions of asthma and illnesses that later came to be known as allergies are found in the writings of the ancient Greeks and in the Hebrew Talmud. The ancient Roman poet Lucretius was probably referring to food allergies when he wrote, "What is one man's meat is another man's rank poison."[1]

In 1552, an Italian physician, Jerome Cardan, was summoned to Edinburgh, Scotland. The archbishop of St. Andrews had suffered from asthma for ten years; no one had been able to help him. Could the Italian doctor advise him? Cardan instructed the archbishop to change his diet, to exercise and sleep regularly, and to get rid of the feathers in his bedding. The archbishop's symptoms were relieved.[2]

In 1565, an Italian physician named Leonardo Botallo described several cases in which otherwise healthy men sneezed and developed itchy noses and headaches after smelling roses.[3] The patient of another sixteenth-century physician was extremely sensitive to cats; yet another doctor reported that a young count's lips swelled when he ate eggs. The first skin test to point to the source of an allergy was performed in 1656, when Dr. Pierre Borel applied some egg to the skin of a patient he suspected to be allergic to eggs. A blister arose on the site where the egg rested, thus confirming the doctor's suspicions.[4]

British farmers coined the phrase "hay fever" in the early 1800s. They thought that the itchy eyes, stuffy noses, and sneezing fits that some people suffered through each hay harvest season were caused by exposure to the hay. In 1819, John Bostock, a physician at the Royal Infirmary in Liverpool, England, wrote the first complete description of hay fever— his own. Since the age of eight, Bostock had suffered from sneezing fits, a runny nose, difficulty in breathing, itchy eyes, and the "blahs" every summer. Bostock knew he did not have a cold, but thought his ailment was somehow related to the temperature.[5]

It was not until 1871 that Charles Blackley, another English physician, showed that the cause of hay fever in England was grass pollen. Blackley, who also suffered from hay fever, collected some grass pollen in the summer and stored it

Dr. John Bostock suffered from hay fever. In 1819, he authored the first known description of this bothersome condition.

in a bottle. In midwinter, he opened the bottle, took a whiff, and immediately suffered an attack of hay fever, with watery eyes, runny nose, and a sneezing fit.[6] Still skeptical, Blackley scratched pollen into his skin. The pollen caused considerable redness and swelling. Blackley was finally convinced. Later, by sending special kite-borne pollen traps high in the sky, he showed that pollen could be carried on air currents five hundred meters above the ground.

A Modern Understanding of Allergies

Louis Pasteur's development of vaccines for cholera, rabies, and anthrax in the early 1880s sparked intense international interest in the phenomenon of immunity. Scientists hoped that a better understanding of immunity could help them control other deadly diseases as well. The first clues that the immune cells might be involved in allergic reactions came not from observing "natural" allergies such as hay fever, but from laboratory experiments.

In 1901, French scientists Paul Portier and Charles Richet were invited to take part in a scientific expedition on the Prince of Monaco's yacht. The Prince and his scientific director suggested that Portier and Richet determine how the Portuguese man-of-war (a kind of jellyfish) captured its prey. Sailors were well aware that even touching the jellyfish's tentacles could bring about sharp pain and fainting. The Prince and his scientific director suspected that the creature released a toxin. Portier and Richet might be able to use this toxin to develop a vaccine that would protect sailors against the man-of-war's sting. While on board the yacht, Portier and Richet showed that the jellyfish indeed released a toxin, and concluded that it might well be possible to develop some kind of specific treatment for jellyfish stings.

The scientists continued to work together on the problem after the cruise was over. Unable to obtain jellyfish in their Paris laboratory, they used instead the toxin of a sea anemone that was abundant along the coast of France. Although large doses of the toxin could kill an animal, very small amounts were harmless. In an attempt to develop a vaccine against the sea anemone toxin, they gave several weak doses of the toxin, over a period of weeks, to several dogs. One of the dogs was named Neptune. The first two doses left Neptune "cheerful," according to their laboratory notebook. But after the third dose, poor Neptune gasped for air, suffered diarrhea, vomited blood, and dragged himself along the floor before losing consciousness. He died less than thirty minutes after receiving the shot. Portier and Richet called this phenomenon *anaphylaxis* (the opposite of *prophylaxis*, the Greek word for "protection").[7]

At about the same time, medical scientists were beginning to take note of a disturbing number of reports of severe, sometimes fatal reactions to recently developed treatments for diphtheria and tetanus.

The bacteria that cause diphtheria produce a toxin. In 1890, the German bacteriologist Emil von Behring and his Japanese colleague Shibasaburo Kitasato showed that injecting very small amounts of diphtheria toxin into experimental animals caused the formation of a substance they called antitoxin. This antitoxin, which was found in the serum (the yellow, watery fluid that remains after cells and other solids are removed from the blood) of the animals, specifically neutralized the diphtheria toxin. The antitoxin, when injected into other animals given a deadly dose of the diphtheria toxin, could prevent the development of the disease.

Von Behring and Kitasato used a similar technique to produce an antitoxin that would neutralize the tetanus toxin. Scientists soon found that these antitoxins could be produced in bulk by injecting horses with diphtheria or tetanus toxin. Horse serum containing diphtheria or tetanus antitoxin became the standard treatments for these deadly diseases. The scientists did not yet understand what the protective substances—which soon became known as antibodies—in the horse serum were. They only knew that this antiserum, as the antitoxin-containing horse serum was called, saved lives.

Sometimes, however, the people who received the horse serum therapy suffered serious side effects: skin rashes, joint pains, vomiting, diarrhea, even death. The fatalities were more common when someone had received more than one dose of antiserum.

Why did horse serum—which, unlike sea anemone toxin, contained no dangerous poisons—cause these reactions? Maurice Arthus, a French scientist, sought to solve the puzzle by repeatedly injecting horse serum just under the skin of rabbits. After a few injections, the rabbits developed inflammation—swelling, redness, heat, and pain—at the site of the injections. This became known as the Arthus reaction. A few years later, two American scientists, Milton Rosenau and John Anderson, showed that repeated injections of horse serum into guinea pigs caused anaphylaxis and death. They suggested that the reaction was triggered when the guinea pig produced antibodies against a "strange proteid" in horse serum.[8] Now it was clear that anaphylaxis could be caused by any foreign protein, toxic or nontoxic.

In 1906, the Austrian pediatrician Clemens von Pirquet and his Hungarian-born colleague Béla Schick showed that this "serum sickness" was caused by an immune response to proteins in the horse serum. At first, this was hard for scientists to believe—the immune system was supposed to do only good! Indeed, von Pirquet wrote, "The conception that antibodies, which should protect against disease, are also responsible for disease, sounds at first absurd."[9] To describe this phenomenon, von Pirquet coined a new word—*Allergie*—from the Greek words *allos* and *ergon*, meaning "altered reaction."

By 1910, scientists linked these laboratory results with two common maladies, hay fever and asthma. Like the reactions found in the laboratory experiments, these two ailments, and later a number of other reactions, were shown to be allergies.

In 1921, German scientists Carl Prausnitz and Heinz Küstner showed—indirectly—that antibodies in the patient's blood were responsible for allergies. The two scientists suspected that antibodies were responsible for Küstner's extraordinary sensitivity to certain kinds of cooked fish.

Because they could not detect any anti-fish antibodies in Küstner's serum (we now know that they were present, but could not be detected by the laboratory methods available at that time), they devised a clever experiment. They injected some of Küstner's serum under the skin of Prausnitz and several other colleagues, none of whom were allergic to fish. A day later, they injected the subjects with a fish extract at the same site, just under the skin.

The results were dramatic: ". . . there developed at the site of injection within ten minutes a very itching wheal [a raised red bump] which rapidly, under our eyes, grew to about four centimeters in diameter. . . . After twenty minutes there developed the syndrome of severe generalized intoxication [itchy hives all over the body, stuffy nose, an irritating cough, and labored breathing]. . . ."[10] Because the scientists knew that antibodies in the serum of Küstner's blood could cause such reactions, they concluded (rightly) that their immune reactions to the fish extract were caused by Küstner's anti-fish antibodies.

Delayed-Type Hypersensitivity Reactions

There was evidence that some allergic reactions were different. In 1890, a well-known German bacteriologist named Robert Koch announced, "I have at last hit upon a substance that has the power of preventing the growth of tubercle bacilli, not only in a test tube, but in the body of an animal."[11] His words were greeted with excitement, for the tubercle bacilli were the bacteria responsible for the disease tuberculosis (TB), a major

21

killer at the time. The substance to which Koch referred was taken from the liquid (called tuberculin) used to grow tubercle bacilli. The liquid contained not the bacteria themselves, but substances made by the bacteria. Unfortunately, he was wrong about the benefits of tuberculin: It neither protected healthy people against future tuberculosis infections nor cured those who already had tuberculosis. In fact, injecting tuberculin into such patients often led to adverse reactions and even death.

Scientists who continued to experiment with tuberculin showed that small amounts of the material injected just under the skin of tuberculosis patients resulted in a local inflammatory reaction. Because people who were not infected with the TB-causing bacteria did not have a reaction to tuberculin, the test could be used to help doctors diagnose the disease. Von Pirquet and other scientists developed refinements of the test that would serve as the basis for the TB test still in use today.

Although researchers soon recognized the reaction as an allergy, there were some significant and puzzling differences from other allergic reactions. The key player in the allergic reaction to tuberculin seemed to be a cell, not an antibody. Immune reactions caused by antibodies—like the anti-fish antibodies in the Prausnitz and Küstner experiment—result in swelling and redness without tissue damage. The tuberculin reaction did cause tissue damage. Furthermore, allergic reactions caused by antibodies began minutes after the immune system encountered the allergen, and faded away after a few hours; the tuberculin-induced reaction began four or five hours after testing, peaking at about forty-eight hours.

Exposure to poison ivy can cause contact dermatitis, an example of a delayed-type hypersensitivity reaction.

This type of allergic reaction eventually came to be known as "delayed-type hypersensitivity." The cells responsible for the reaction are a type of lymphocyte (white blood cells) called T cells. Contact dermatitis—a type of skin allergy to substances such as poison ivy or nickel—is an example of delayed-type hypersensitivity reaction.

Allergy Drugs and Immunotherapy

In 1911, a British scientist, Leonard Noon, tried to develop a new treatment for hay fever. He believed—wrongly—that pollen contained a toxin responsible for the symptoms of hay fever. Like Richet and Portier before him, he thought that repeated injections of very small amounts of pollen extracts might induce the body to make anti-pollen antibodies. Although his theory was wrong for pollen, the method of treatment showed promise for other allergens. Scientists began to experiment with injections of watered-down extracts of other allergy-causing substances. These injections became known as allergy shots. Allergy shots are now used, with varying degrees of success, to treat people who have severe allergies to insect venom, pollen, and animals.

In 1910, a British scientist named Sir Henry Dale was studying a fungus that grew on rye plants. He isolated a chemical, which came to be called histamine, from the fungus. Further research showed that injecting this chemical into experimental animals caused a reaction very much like anaphylactic shock. In 1932, German scientist Wilhelm Feldberg and American scientist Carl Albert Draystedt showed that histamine is released by cells during an allergic reaction involving antibodies. This set the stage for the development of antihistamines, drugs that could block the action of histamine. Antihistamines were the first really effective treatment for many allergies. Daniel Bovet, a Swiss researcher, developed the first antihistamine drug in 1937, and later won a Nobel Prize for his work.

In the 1920s, scientists were able to show that the tendency to develop allergies, especially hay fever and asthma, is genetically inherited. Two early American pioneers in the new clinical specialty of allergy, Arthur F. Coca and Robert A. Cooke, coined the term *atopy* to describe the features of genetically determined allergic conditions. (People who have a genetic tendency to develop allergies are said to be atopic.) The team classified many allergic reactions in humans.

Although researchers now had a general idea of the cause of allergies, and methods to diagnose and treat allergies, it was not until the 1960s that scientists worked out the details of the allergic reaction, described in the next chapter. Only now are scientists beginning to answer the question that has plagued allergy sufferers throughout the ages: "Why me?"

3

What Are Allergies?

Mold spores, weed pollens, and grass pollens all give President Bill Clinton watery, itchy eyes and a runny or stuffy nose. Even Socks, the First Cat, makes him sneeze.

Jane's first taste of yogurt—at the age of ten months—made her vomit, wheeze, and clutch at her throat, unable to breathe. Jane is now a healthy young girl, as long as she avoids milk and eggs. She is matter-of-fact about her condition: "Milk is bad news for me, but I love vegetables," she explains.[1]

Sarah breaks out in an itchy rash whenever she touches any metal object with nickel in it. She has learned to recognize and avoid potential sources of nickel: zippers, buckles, buttons, coins, scissors, needles, and jewelry, including fourteen-karat gold items.[2]

On the surface, President Clinton, Jane, and Sarah appear to have very different conditions. In fact, all of their ailments are caused by allergies. Allergies occur when the immune system, whose purpose is to defend the body against harmful invaders, attacks something—called an allergen—which is not really harmful. The symptoms of their allergies vary, depending on the site of the allergic reaction. In President Clinton's case, the reaction takes place in his nose and throat. Jane's allergic reaction occurs in her digestive system and then spreads throughout her body, while Sarah's reaction happens just under the skin.

The War Within: The Immune System Versus Disease

To understand allergies, we need to know something about the immune system itself. An individual's immune system is superbly equipped to recognize, destroy, and remember disease-causing microbes. Microbes are microscopic organisms such as bacteria and viruses. These invaders, indeed any foreign substance, have proteins that identify them as "non-self"—that is, not belonging in the body. These proteins are called antigens, and each invader carries antigens that are unique to it. When the immune system recognizes an antigen, it sends in a whole army of white blood cells to repel the invader.

Some of the first white blood cells on the scene are the phagocytes—cells that surround and destroy antigens. One very important type of phagocyte, called the macrophage, takes the process a step farther. The macrophages display pieces of some of the antigen proteins on their surface, much

27

as a raccoon hunter might wear a coonskin cap (see Figure 1). The antigen pieces on the macrophages help to "turn on" another important type of white blood cell, the helper T cell. The helper T cell attaches to the antigen on the surface of the macrophage. It then releases chemicals that stimulate yet another kind of white blood cell: the B cell.

B cells produce many copies of a Y-shaped protein called an antibody (also called an immunoglobulin). It is easy to think of the antibody as having one leg that points down and two arms that reach outward. Each arm of the antibody recognizes and binds to only one antigen. B cells carry many copies of this antibody on their surface. When a B cell receives the stimulating chemical from a helper T cell *and* recognizes an antigen, it springs into action. It makes billions of new copies of its trademark antibody and releases them into the

The dander of some pets causes an allergic reaction in some individuals.

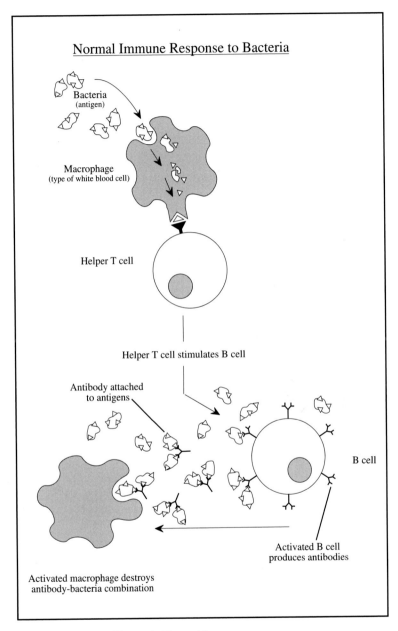

Figure 1: Normal immune response

bloodstream. These roving antibodies help neutralize the antigen and make it easier for macrophages to destroy the invader.

There are five classes of antibodies, or immunoglobulins: IgA, IgD, IgE, IgG, and IgM. Each class is distinguished by the structure of its leg and the role it plays in the immune response. In the normal course of an immune response, a B cell produces an IgM antibody first, then switches to the longer-lived IgG.

Antibodies do not last forever, but a small number of the antigen-recognizing T cells and B cells are changed into long-lived memory cells. These memory cells circulate in the blood or stay in the lymph nodes, waiting for the next time the same antigen enters the body. When this happens, they respond very quickly and vigorously. They can often rid the body of an organism before it has a chance to cause problems.

IgE Antibodies Cause Allergy Symptoms

A great many foreign substances enter our bodies every day: dust, pollen, food, smoke, smog, you name it. Most are relatively harmless, and just as the garbage collector comes before dawn to haul off the trash, our immune systems generally clean away the collected debris so effortlessly that we never even notice it. People with allergies, on the other hand, might call out the anti-parasite patrol for a harmless piece of dust. When harmless antigens provoke an allergic response, we call them allergens.

The first stage of an allergic reaction, *sensitization*, is silent (see Figure 2). When an allergen such as pollen enters the body, the immune system initially responds just as it would to any invading organism. The macrophages gobble up the pollen, display pieces of it on their surface, and send out chemical signals to recruit helper T cells. After the initial response, however, a special subset of helper T cells, called TH2, produce a chemical signal called interleukin 4 (IL4). IL4 tells the B cells to produce IgE, not the usual IgG, antibodies. IgE is the antibody responsible for allergies. People with allergies have an unusually high number of TH2 cells and elevated levels of IL4.

By this time, days or weeks may have passed since the first encounter with the allergen. It has come and gone unnoticed by the person—but not by the immune system! The IgE molecules attach themselves to special receptors on two types of immune cells: mast cells and basophils. Mast cells generally stay

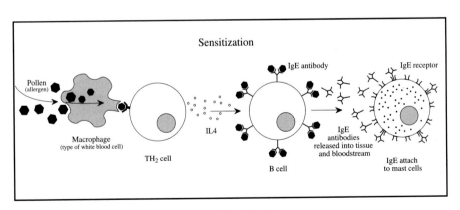

Figure 2: Sensitization

close to blood vessels and the epithelium—the layer of cells covering surfaces that make contact with the outside world, such as the skin and the linings of the respiratory and digestive tracts. Basophils circulate throughout the bloodstream.

In people with allergies, the mast cells and basophils are loaded with IgE antibodies that lie in wait for the next encounter with that same allergen. And they can wait a long, long time: months or even years.

After just one exposure or hundreds of exposures to the allergen (the sensitization period can vary greatly, depending on the zeal with which B cells produce IgE), the stage is set for the next part of an allergic reaction: the activation of mast cells (see Figure 3). The next time the sensitizing allergen enters the body, it binds to IgE molecules on mast cells. A single allergen molecule attached to two different IgE molecules side-by-side on a mast cell induces the cell to release a combination of potent chemicals that, directly or indirectly, cause the symptoms of allergy.

Perhaps the most well known of these chemicals is histamine, which causes cells in the epithelium to secrete mucus. Histamine makes the smooth muscles of the airways and intestines contract, and can cause small blood vessels to become leaky, leading to redness and swelling. Mast cells also release fat molecules, similar in action to histamine but longer lasting, and chemicals that are toxic to other cells.

This second stage of the allergic reaction can take place just a few minutes after the allergen enters the body. But there is often a third, longer-lasting phase to the allergic reaction.

Mast cells recruit basophils, T cells, and other immune cells into the surrounding tissue. These newcomers release still more chemicals that extend and intensify the early symptoms, sometimes damaging local tissue. They contribute to the chronic inflammation that plagues many sufferers of hay fever and asthma long after the allergen is gone.

The tendency to develop allergies is inherited, not contagious. If one parent has allergies, the odds are one in three that the child will also develop allergies (although not necessarily the same ones). If both parents have allergies, the child will almost certainly develop them. There is some evidence that parents can carry a genetic trait for allergies without actually having an allergy themselves—35 percent of allergy-free parents have children with allergies.[3] People who have a genetic tendency to develop allergies will often react to more than one substance.

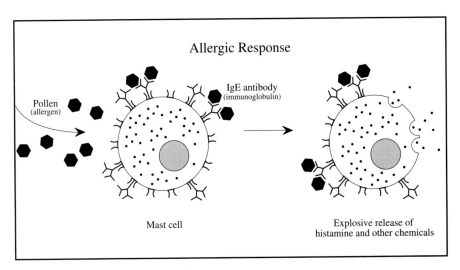

Figure 3: Activation

Why Do We Have IgE Antibodies?

Many scientists believe that the allergic response originally evolved to help us fight parasites. People who inherited the tendency to produce high levels of IgE would have enjoyed an evolutionary advantage over those who produced low levels. Those who live in developing countries, where poor sanitation often results in high parasite levels, still rely upon IgE antibodies to help their immune systems keep unwelcome guests at least partly under control.

Where people are regularly exposed to parasites, IgE antibodies specific for parasite proteins may occupy all of the available IgE binding sites on mast cells and basophils. In this case, it is less likely that allergen-specific antibodies could activate these cells. Eric Ottesen, a parasitologist and allergist at the National Institute of Allergy and Infectious Diseases, points out that allergies are rare in developing countries where parasites are common. He notes that in several instances where public health measures helped reduce parasitic infections, allergy cases have soared.[4]

Allergic Rhinitis

By far the most common allergy is allergic rhinitis. Allergic rhinitis is popularly but inaccurately known as hay fever (it is not caused by hay, and it does not cause a fever). Allergic rhinitis is an inflammation of the mucous membrane of the nose. Airborne microscopic allergens trapped by mucus and hairs on the inside of the nose cause mast cells in the mucous membranes to release histamine. This makes the tissues inside the nose, sinuses, eyelids, and eyes swell and become inflamed. The symptoms are violent sneezing, a stuffy or runny nose, watery eyes, and an itchy feeling in the nose and throat and on the roof of the mouth.

For many, springtime signals the beginning of the sneezing season. These people have seasonal allergic rhinitis, triggered by pollen. Flowers generally produce large, sticky grains of pollen, and rely upon bees and other insects to spread the pollen from plant to plant. These particles are usually harmless. However, the tiny, light, dry grains of pollen produced by grass, weeds, shrubs, and trees can be potent allergens. The ragweed plant, responsible for most allergies in the United States, can produce one million grains of pollen each season. There is seemingly no getting away from it, either. Ragweed pollen can be carried by wind currents to a distance of four hundred miles. It can enter houses through tiny cracks, screens, and even window air conditioners. As few as twenty pollen grains per cubic meter can provoke an allergic response.[5]

Although pollen counts drop on warm, humid days, these conditions are ideal for another common allergen: mold spores. Molds are microscopic fungi, and although they are not plants, their reproductive cells, or spores, float through the air like pollen. Molds thrive on grains, rotting logs, dead leaves, and grass cuttings. They usually appear in the spring, reach their peak on warm, humid summer days, and disappear with the first frost (although the spores themselves can linger until the first snowfall).

For some people, the sneezing, sniffling, and congestion last all year. People who have year-round allergic rhinitis are sensitive to airborne particles found inside buildings. Household dust contains a variety of unsavory allergens. Among the worst offenders are dust mites (their Latin name, *Dermatophagoides,* means that they live on flakes of human skin)—or more accurately, their feces, which are about the same size as grains of pollen.

Cockroach body parts are another common house dust allergen. Households with pets add yet another component to the mix: pet dander, or flaked-off skin cells. Dander is actually the carrier of several major allergens found in saliva, in urine, and on skin cells. Indoor molds, like their outdoor cousins, often produce allergenic spores. The molds thrive in bathrooms, damp basements and closets, and in upholstered furniture, mattresses, old books, and humidifiers.

Asthma

"Asthma" is derived from the Greek word for panting, or breathlessness. This breathlessness, and a feeling of tightness in the chest, wheezing, and coughing, are all classic signs of asthma. These symptoms can be very mild or quite severe. Here is one description of what it feels like to have asthma: Take a deep breath, and hold it for a minute. Now, breathe in at the top of your lungs and do not let out any air. Many asthmatics say, "My breath does not go out all the way." This is little wonder, as asthmatics trap as much air in their chests as there is in a basketball.[6] Asthma attacks can last minutes, hours, or even days.

Although asthma, like allergic rhinitis, is a respiratory ailment, it is much more serious and sometimes even deadly. People who have asthma should be under the regular care of a doctor. During normal breathing, the airways, or bronchi, are always open, allowing air to move freely in and out of the lungs. But during an asthma attack, these airways swell and tighten, and the cells lining the airways produce too much mucus. The result is that it is difficult to breathe out.

Allergens are the most common asthma triggers, especially in young people. About 90 percent of asthmatics younger than sixteen have an allergic component to their illness. That number drops to 70 percent for asthmatics younger than thirty, and to 50 percent for asthmatics older than thirty.[7] Many of the same airborne allergens that plague people with allergic rhinitis also cause asthma attacks: animal dander, dust mites, pollen, and mold spores. Food allergens can also cause severe asthma, as can latex. But asthma can also be triggered by exercise, cold air, sulfites used as food preservatives, aspirin and other similar drugs, air pollution, perfumes or other odors, smoking or secondhand smoke, viral infection, and even laughing! Stress and depression, although they do not trigger asthma by themselves, may make an existing situation even worse.

The symptoms of allergy-induced asthma arise when IgE antibodies on the surface of mast cells in the bronchi bind to allergens, triggering the release of histamine. Asthma attacks, like other allergic reactions, often have an early, immediate phase and a late, long-lasting phase. The early-phase reaction, which begins just after exposure to the allergen and peaks within half an hour, can be frightening in its suddenness and severity, but it responds well to drugs that relax the airways. Yet these drugs, useful as they are, do not treat the effects of the late-phase reaction: bronchial inflammation and the over-production of mucus. Late-phase asthma reactions are harder to treat, and they can be deadly. In fact, many deaths from asthma can be traced to late-phase reactions that were left untreated.

The Plants That Make Us Sneeze

Ragweed is the major source of allergy-producing weed pollen in North America. Other significant sources include sagebrush, redroot pigweed, careless weed, spiny amaranth, tumbleweed, burning bush, and English plantain. Some troublesome grass pollens are timothy, redtop, Bermuda grass, orchard grass, sweet vernal, ryegrass, and some bluegrasses. Almost every popular tree produces allergenic pollens: elm, maple, oak, ash, birch, poplar, pecan, cottonwood, and mountain cedar.

Anaphylaxis

An allergic reaction that occurs not just in one organ system—the respiratory system, for example—but in many organs or tissues throughout the body can be very dangerous. This type of reaction is called anaphylaxis. Although allergic reactions that are confined to a specific tissue or organ are technically a kind of local anaphylactic reaction, the term *anaphylaxis* is usually reserved for a reaction that occurs throughout the body.

Anaphylaxis may be triggered by allergies to certain foods, drugs, or insect venom. In recent years, latex—derived from the milky sap of a rubber tree—has been responsible for an increasing number of anaphylactic reactions, particularly among health care workers who frequently come in contact with latex.

Anaphylaxis is caused by the explosive release of histamine from mast cells throughout the body, seconds to minutes after exposure to the allergen. Histamine released throughout the body causes blood vessels to become dilated and leak blood fluids. This can lead to a drastic drop in blood pressure, which in turn may cause shock (a condition characterized by racing pulse, weakness, paleness, confusion, and unconsciousness) and potentially fatal heart attacks. There may be intestinal cramps and diarrhea. The lips, tongue, larynx, and throat may swell, causing difficulty in breathing or even suffocation.

Severe anaphylaxis can often be reversed with emergency treatment, but anyone who has had a mild anaphylactic reaction is in danger of having a severe one next time. The very best treatment is to avoid the allergen if possible. Fortunately, the total number of deaths from anaphylaxis in the United States is low, about one for every 2.5 million people each year.[8]

Insect Stings

For most people, a bee sting is painful but not particularly alarming. Toxic proteins in the bee's venom may cause the area to turn red, swell, and itch, but the discomfort does not last long. But some develop allergies to the venom proteins. Because insects inject the allergen directly into the bloodstream, allowing it to circulate throughout the body,

One sting from a bee can be extremely dangerous to some people. Anaphylaxis may result from an allergy to insect venom.

allergies to insect venom are the most common cause of anaphylaxis. In the United States alone, at least forty people each year die from anaphylactic reactions to insect venom, although that estimate is probably low. Scientists believe that up to 5 percent of the population may be allergic to the venom of one or more stinging insects.[9]

Stinging insects in the order Hymenoptera account for most allergic reactions. Honeybees, bumblebees, hornets, wasps, yellow jackets, and fire ants are all in this order. Of these, yellow jackets cause the most allergic reactions. They nest in the ground or in walls, and are frequently disturbed by lawn mowing, gardening, and other outdoor activities. They love sweets, and often hover around outdoor picnickers and garbage cans. Honeybees and bumblebees are normally docile. Beekeepers, who frequently disturb beehives, run the greatest risk of bee stings. If you are allergic to the venom of one insect, there is a good chance you will also be allergic to the venom of another closely related insect (this is especially true of yellow jackets and hornets).

Not all allergic reactions to insect stings are anaphylactic. People with mild allergies to insect venom may develop itchy eyes and hives. Whatever symptoms occur usually do so within a few minutes, although they may not appear for hours or even days. Delayed symptoms include fever, painful joints, hives, and swollen lymph glands. Generally, the sooner the reaction occurs, the more severe it will be.

Food Allergies

An allergic reaction to an insect sting is one thing, but an allergy to a favorite food is quite another. It just does not seem fair. Fortunately, only about 2 to 8 percent of children and 2 percent of adults have true food allergies. Most food allergies are triggered by peanuts, tree nuts, cow's milk, egg whites, wheat, soy products, fish, or shellfish. Scientists believe that children are more likely to have food allergies because their immune and digestive systems are not yet fully developed. Many, but not all, children will outgrow their food allergies, although allergies to peanuts, tree nuts, fish, or shellfish are usually lifelong. These foods also commonly cause the most severe reactions.

Food allergies, like all the other allergies described thus far, are caused by IgE antibodies and the release of histamine from mast cells. The allergic reaction may take place in the mouth, resulting in a swollen tongue or lips. If it takes place in the digestive tract, it causes stomach cramps, vomiting, and diarrhea. Sensitized mast cells under the skin may cause hives, rashes, or eczema. Recent studies have shown that food allergies can also contribute to asthma attacks.[10]

Anaphylactic reactions to a food allergen may start within minutes of eating even tiny amounts of food. These reactions are rare, but they appear to be increasing. In fact, food allergies in general are becoming more common—perhaps due to changes in food habits. It has become common practice, for example, to give young children peanut butter and jelly sandwiches, and scientists say that peanut allergies are indeed on the rise. We eat more processed foods, which often contain allergenic protein additives such as milk or soy. Eating out has become increasingly common. It is hard for the allergic diner to know exactly what goes into every dish.

It is important to distinguish food allergies from food intolerances. Lactose intolerance, for example, is sometimes mistaken for milk allergy. Many people of African, Hispanic, or Mediterranean origin lack an enzyme that helps them digest lactose, a sugar found in milk products. They may get cramps and diarrhea when they eat or drink products that contain lactose. Although people with true food allergies must completely avoid their allergens, those with food intolerances can often eat small amounts of the offending food without any problem.

Drug Allergies

The development of modern drugs has helped us live longer, healthier lives. But a small percentage of people are allergic to certain drugs. Typical symptoms of drug allergies include an itchy feeling, hives, a rash, nausea, or vomiting. Some allergic reactions may develop days or even weeks after the drug is given, and subside gradually after the drug is cleared from the body. Some drugs, especially aspirin and related medicines, can trigger asthma attacks.

The penicillin drugs, some of the most widely used antibiotics, are also among the most notorious drug allergens. Scientists estimate that one of every fifty people given a penicillin drug has an allergic reaction—usually not life-threatening. Only about 2 percent of allergic reactions to penicillin drugs result in anaphylaxis, but because these drugs are so widely used, they account for 75 percent of all deaths from anaphylaxis in the United States.[11]

Latex Allergy

Latex is used in surgical gloves, condoms, diaphragms, balloons, underwear—just about any product that is rubbery or stretchy. Sometimes it is even in the air. It may be carried on the cornstarch particles used to ease surgical gloves on and off, or perhaps shed from automobile tires on the freeway.[12] Allergy to latex—virtually unheard of in 1988—has become an increasing public health concern for health care workers.

In 1987, the Centers for Disease Control (CDC) recommended that all health care workers wear surgical gloves to protect themselves against AIDS and other blood-borne infections. Emergency medical technicians, nurses, doctors, dentists, and their assistants began wearing latex gloves more often, for longer periods of time. With the skyrocketing demand for latex products, hundreds of new latex manufacturing plants sprang up, and in the opinion of many, quality was sacrificed for quantity. Many of the new latex products contained more of the allergenic proteins.[13]

Although rare in the general population, latex allergy affects an estimated 5 to 41 percent of health care workers who wear latex gloves much of the day. A staggering 20 to 60 percent of children with spina bifida, a birth defect in which the spinal column is not properly closed, have latex allergy. These children have many surgical procedures, usually involving exposure to latex. People who have other IgE-mediated allergies, especially asthma, allergic rhinitis, or food allergy, are more likely to develop latex allergy. Some of the proteins found in certain foods, especially bananas, avocados, and chestnuts, "look" like latex proteins to the immune system. Antibodies to these foods may also react to latex proteins, so people who have these food allergies may also be allergic to latex.

The most common allergic reactions to latex include contact dermatitis, allergic rhinitis, and asthma. But people with a

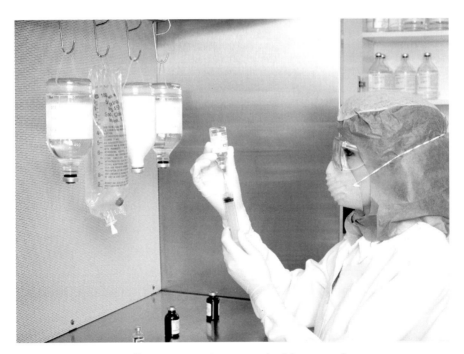

Latex allergy is increasing among health care workers.

severe allergy to latex can have anaphylactic reactions to even small amounts of latex.

Skin Allergies

Skin allergies come in many forms and, like allergic rhinitis, are fairly common. Scientists estimate that one in five Americans has had hives at one time or another. A related condition is angioedema, which involves swelling well below the surface of the skin, especially around the eyes and lips but also on the hands, feet, and throat. As might be expected, the symptoms of hives and angioedema are triggered when IgE-studded mast cells in or just under the skin latch onto allergens. The release of histamine and other chemicals causes blood vessels to swell and leak.

An attack of hives or angioedema may be brought on by an allergic reaction to all sorts of substances and conditions: foods, drugs, insect bites, infections, animal dander, pollen, cold, heat, light, and emotional distress. Couch potatoes who claim to be "allergic to exercise" may not know that some people really do break out in hives after exercising, sometimes in combination with eating certain foods. Often, it is hard to pinpoint the cause. The attacks can last anywhere from hours to weeks. Although short-lived attacks are relatively harmless, they may signal the development of a more dangerous sensitivity to a substance that could lead to anaphylaxis.

Another common skin allergy is atopic dermatitis, more commonly known as eczema. The hallmarks of eczema are patches of dry, extremely itchy, thickened skin. Doctors call it "the itch that rashes."[14] Eczema is most common in babies and children, although it can occur at any time of life. About 1 to 3 percent of infants and children have eczema at one time or another, and although most outgrow it as they get older, they are very likely to develop allergic rhinitis, asthma, or both.

While scientists are not sure what causes eczema, there is good evidence that allergies are involved. The tendency to develop eczema is inherited from the parents, and most people with eczema have a close family member with asthma, eczema, or allergic rhinitis. Eczema is often triggered by food and environmental allergies. Most people with eczema have very high levels of IgE in their blood. They may have abnormal white blood cells, abnormal blood flow to the skin, and a tendency to develop viral and bacterial skin infections. Stress may make the symptoms worse. President Lyndon B. Johnson apparently suffered from an eczema-like rash on his hands, especially when he was tense and unhappy.

Certain chemicals that come into contact with the skin sometimes provoke an itchy red rash, often accompanied by swelling, bumps, and blisters. This common condition, known as contact dermatitis, affects millions of people each year—in fact, it accounts for 30 percent of all work-related illnesses.[15] Contact dermatitis can cause pain and discomfort, especially if the blisters burst and become infected, but it has no lasting effects. Some cases of contact dermatitis are caused by an allergic response to certain chemicals; other cases are caused simply by a chemical's toxic effect on skin cells.

In either situation, potential offending chemicals are all around us: in nickel and rubber compounds, cement, paper, leather, timber, and household detergents. Some people may be allergic to printer's ink, hair, or fur dyes. Others may react to skin creams, cosmetics, nail polish, perfumes, or eyedrop solutions. Drugs that are placed on the skin, such as ointments, may cause an allergic response. About half of all people are allergic to urushiol, an oily compound in poison ivy, oak, and sumac. Although it takes only a tiny amount of urushiol to provoke a reaction, direct contact—by brushing up against poison ivy, or even touching a pet or clothing that has brushed up against poison ivy—is necessary.

Allergic contact dermatitis, unlike most other allergies, is not caused by IgE antibodies. Instead, it is caused by T cells and phagocytes, which release a variety of toxic chemicals into the surrounding tissue. It is an example of a delayed-type hypersensitivity reaction (described in Chapter 2). The rash peaks at about five days, and disappears within one or two weeks unless contact with the allergen continues. Like the IgE-mediated response, the delayed-type hypersensitivity response also plays a role in combating harmful invaders, most notably the bacteria that cause tuberculosis.

What Allergies Are *Not*: Multiple Chemical Sensitivity and Other Unproven Theories

Marilyn and Richard could not get a good night's sleep. They blamed the formaldehyde in their mattress for their nightly headaches, watery eyes, itchy noses, and dry throats.[16] They are among the millions of Americans who believe they are allergic to many of the chemicals in the modern environment—including normally harmless levels of food additives, synthetic fabrics, perfumes, trace contaminants in water, household cleaners, and glues. People who are sensitive to such chemicals may have other common complaints, including fatigue, headache, dizziness, depression, and impaired concentration. They may visit many physicians, only to be told again and again that there is nothing wrong with them.

In fact, there *is* something wrong. Their symptoms are real, and the name of their ailment is multiple chemical sensitivity (MCS). But there is much dispute among medical scientists regarding the cause of MCS. A branch of allergists on the fringe of the medical community, called clinical ecologists or environmental medicine specialists, believe that overexposure to one substance leads to an allergic sensitivity to many environmental factors. They often prescribe treatments that require major changes in the home, diet, and lifestyle of the patient.

There is no scientific evidence to support the clinical ecologists' claims or treatments. Major medical organizations, including the American Academy of Allergy, Asthma and Immunology and the American College of Physicians, do not support the claims or treatments of clinical ecologists.[17] Most medical scientists believe that MCS is triggered by emotional stress, and is, therefore, most effectively treated by psychiatric therapy.

There is also a theory that a common yeast called *Candida albicans* causes allergies. *Candida*, which is normally present in the body, can sometimes grow out of control after a person has taken antibiotics. It is a common cause of vaginal infections in women and, some people believe, can impair the immune system. The theory holds that *Candida* allergies are responsible for a variety of symptoms, including fatigue, hyperactivity, headaches, and even flatulence. There is no scientific evidence to support this theory.[18]

4
Diagnosing Allergies

Many people go through their entire lives without knowing that their sneezing, sniffling, and runny noses are caused not by frequent colds, but by hay fever. A woman may not link the itchy red rash she occasionally develops with wearing Great-aunt Mathilda's costume jewelry.

There are some telltale signs that can help people know when they are dealing with allergies. Do coldlike symptoms regularly occur at certain seasons of the year? Are they worse on the nights when the cat sleeps on the bed? Do they sometimes last for weeks? Positive answers to any of these questions may mean that the person has an allergy. Those with mild allergies often either ignore them or keep them under control with over-the-counter drugs.

The nickel in some costume jewelry can cause contact dermatitis.

Some people, however, have severe allergies that interfere with their day-to-day life. These people—as well as those who have asthma, and those who develop hives or an itchy rash after eating certain foods, being stung by an insect, or taking a drug—should see a doctor, preferably a board-certified allergist. People with serious symptoms—a severe asthma attack or anaphylaxis—should go to the emergency room immediately and schedule an appointment with a doctor later.

The doctor can usually identify the offending allergen or allergens, and advise patients on how to avoid them. In many cases, this is the easiest and cheapest form of treatment. The doctor may be able to prescribe drugs that work better than over-the-counter medications. The patient may be a candidate for allergy shots (immunotherapy).

It is important to take some care in choosing an allergist. There are too many practitioners who use unsound methods to diagnose nonexistent allergies in order to prescribe long, expensive, and often questionable treatments (see "Do Not Trust These Tests!"). It is best to get a recommendation for an allergist from a competent nurse, physician, or pharmacist. The associations listed at the back of this book (see "For More Information") provide information on reputable allergists and allergy clinics.

A Visit to the Allergist: What to Expect

Ten-year-old Erika Weiberg has inherited her father's light-brown hair, his love of sports, and his allergies. Allergies to grass, tree, and weed pollens plague Erika's father, Kevin Weiberg, from the spring through the fall. Dust mites and molds take up the slack—to a lesser extent—in the winter. He is well acquainted with the symptoms: sneezing, sniffling, and watery, itchy eyes. As a child, he loved sports, but he often had to sit on the sidelines and watch his teammates play while he nursed yet another allergy-associated ear infection. So when Erika, at the age of six, began to get a series of "colds" that would not go away, Erika's father suspected that his daughter had allergies as well. Her parents made an appointment with the family's allergist, who found that Erika is allergic to pollens, molds, pet dander, and dust mites.[1]

The first visit to the allergist may take two or three hours, or it may be split into two or three shorter visits. The doctor will do three things: interview the patient, do a physical examination, and run a variety of laboratory and allergy tests. The patient interview is by far the most important part of the allergist's diagnostic tool kit.

Here are some of the questions allergists ask their patients: What is the chief complaint? How does it feel? When do you notice it most? Do you have any present or past medical problems? Does anyone in your family have allergies? Where do you work, live, and play? Do you have pets, and if so, where do they sleep? Do you use a feather pillow or down comforter? Do you have a damp basement? What kind of soap or cosmetics do you use? Do you do yard work? Do you ever feel sick after eating certain foods?[2]

Next, the doctor takes a close look at the patient's skin, eyes, nose, ears, lungs, and abdomen. The doctor is looking for characteristic signs of allergies: a pale gray-blue, soggy lining inside the nose is typical of people with allergic rhinitis, for example. Sometimes the doctor may find another cause altogether for the symptoms: One little girl suspected of having a bad summer cold or allergy had a piece of cotton lodged up her nose. She simply had an infection.[3]

The doctor may order X rays and blood, urine, or other tests to rule out the possibility of other diseases. Chronic bronchitis (an infection of the bronchial tubes) or pneumonia may masquerade as allergies. In adults, especially those who smoke, the doctors might look for emphysema. Children may be

Do Not Trust These Tests!

A number of other tests are considered ineffective or unreliable by most mainstream doctors or by the American Academy of Allergy, Asthma and Immunology. One, called cytotoxic testing, is based on the claim that adding a specific allergen to a sample of the patient's blood will result in a reduction or change in the white blood cells if the patient is allergic.

Another, the Rinkel method, claims to reveal not only specific allergies, but the best dosage for allergy shots as well, by injecting varying strengths of the allergen just under the skin and measuring the skin reaction. While the Rinkel method can establish a patient's allergies to ragweed, it is not an effective guide to treatment doses.

Provocative and neutralization testing is based on the injection of a tiny amount of the suspected allergen into the skin; if the patient reports feeling ill, a "neutralizing solution" (a diluted form of the allergen extract) is given. A variation of this technique is to place drops of the suspected food allergen under the patient's tongue and watch for signs of illness.[4]

Finally, run, do not walk, from anyone who claims to make an allergy diagnosis by analyzing the patient's hair; using an electronic device to measure the "energy" produced by certain foods; using a dowsing rod or pendulum; or measuring the patient's muscle strength as he or she grips a vial of the suspected allergen. These tests are scientifically unsound.

tested for cystic fibrosis, a disease that causes cells lining the lung to produce too much mucus. A parasitic infection may induce hives or asthma.

Any patient who complains of a frequent cough or breathing problems will be asked to do a bronchial challenge test. This requires breathing into a machine that measures the lungs' ability to move air in and out. Most people are able to exhale 80 percent of the air in their lungs in one second; exhaling less than 80 percent may indicate asthma, especially if a drug that expands bronchial passages improves performance.

The most commonly used allergy test is the skin prick test. It is especially useful for determining respiratory, penicillin, and insect bite allergies. The doctor or nurse usually places a drop of each suspected allergen on the skin, and then lightly scratches or pricks the skin. Sometimes a tiny amount of allergen is injected directly into the skin. After fifteen or twenty minutes, the doctor will check the test sites. If there is swelling and redness at the site, the patient has IgE antibodies to that allergen.

The skin prick test, although valuable, is not foolproof. It is not uncommon for a patient to have a positive skin response to an allergen that has not made the patient sick in the past. Also, a negative skin response does not always mean that the patient is not sensitive to that allergen. This is why the medical history is such an important part of allergy testing.

Testing for contact dermatitis calls for a different approach—the skin patch test. The doctor or nurse will put a variety of the common or suspected culprits directly onto the

Do I Have Asthma?

It is important for people who have asthma to be under the care of a doctor. A "yes" answer to any of these questions suggests that you may have asthma and should see a qualified allergist or doctor.[5]

In the past twelve months . . .

- Have you had one or more sudden severe episodes of coughing, wheezing (high-pitched sounds when breathing out), or shortness of breath?

- Have you had colds that "go to the chest" or take more than ten days to get over?

- Have you had coughing, wheezing, or shortness of breath during a particular season or time of the year?

- Have you used any medications that help you breathe better? Do the medications relieve the symptoms?

In the past four weeks, have you had coughing, wheezing, or shortness of breath . . .

- At night that has awakened you?

- In the early morning?

- After running, moderate exercise, or other physical activity?

skin and cover the areas with patches. After forty-eight hours, the patches are removed. A rash under any of the patches is usually enough to identify the offending allergen.[6]

Skin tests are not as accurate for food allergies. If the patient is suspected of having a food allergy, the doctor may order a double-blind food challenge test, considered the "gold standard" for diagnosing food allergies.[7] One day, the patient is given a capsule containing the allergen; another day, a

Patients diagnosed with asthma may need to use an inhaler. The inhaler allows the patient to obtain medicine, called bronchodilators, which provides quick relief to most individuals.

placebo capsule. The placebo—an inactive substance used as a control, or comparison—is an important part of the experiment because the patient's attitudes about a suspected allergen can often affect the outcome of this test. It is called "double-blind" because neither the doctor nor the patient knows which pill is which, until the test is over. If the allergen-containing pill (but not the placebo) triggers symptoms, the patient is probably allergic to that food.

Sometimes skin or challenge tests cannot—or should not—be done. Skin testing is difficult with very young children or people with skin disorders such as eczema. It is not useful if the patient has been taking antihistamines. People who have a history of life-threatening allergic reactions should never take skin or challenge tests. In this case, a laboratory test called the radioallergosorbent test (RAST) can be used instead. The doctor or nurse takes a sample of the patient's blood and sends it to the laboratory, where technicians can detect IgE antibodies to specific allergens. Although the RAST is a simple test, it is usually not as sensitive as the skin prick test. It is also slower and more expensive.

Clearly, diagnosing allergies is a difficult and complex process. RAST should never be the only diagnostic tool. Beware of mail-order companies that claim to diagnose allergies from a sample of the patient's blood. In 1985, scientists from the Food and Drug Administration sent a sample of cow's blood to a testing lab that claimed to identify allergy-provoking foods for $350. The lab's diagnosis: the "patient" was allergic to milk![8]

5

Preventing Allergies

Richard Schneider's nose was constantly congested, so much that his mother thought he might need an operation. As it turned out, Richard has allergies—to certain foods, plants, molds, and pet dander. Richard's mother removed the offending foods from Richard's diet and put the dogs and cats outside the house. Now, unless he eats the wrong foods or lets his pets sleep inside his room, Richard breathes normally.[1]

Like many people, Richard is able to keep his allergies under control by avoiding, or at least reducing his exposure to, the allergens that make him sick. This is the first line of "treatment" suggested by most allergists. There are no side effects, and it is cheaper than taking allergy shots or medicines over long periods. But avoiding allergens is sometimes harder than it sounds: How does the asthmatic avoid breathing pollen-laden air in the summertime? How do we detect hidden allergens in processed foods? Here are some specific tips for avoiding common allergens.

Avoiding Indoor Allergens

Efforts to make buildings more energy-efficient—by putting up weather stripping or storm windows, for example—prevent cold air from coming in and warm air from escaping. They also prevent house dust—which can contain tiny pieces of dust mites, molds, cockroaches, pet dander, and feathers—from escaping. Considering that Americans spend 90 percent of their time indoors, it is no surprise that these indoor allergens are a major cause of allergies, especially allergic rhinitis, asthma, and allergic skin diseases. Allergies to dust mites and cat dander increase the risk of childhood asthma four to six times.[2]

Allergy-prone people can take a number of steps to reduce house dust and other allergens in their homes. Because people spend about one third of the day sleeping, the first place to start is in the bedroom. Cover mattresses and pillows with plastic or allergen-proof casings, and wash the bedding every week in hot water (cool water does not kill dust mites). Do not use feather pillows, a down comforter, or a wool blanket. Keep cats and dogs out of the bedroom at all times.

In fact, most allergists advise people who are allergic to their pets to give them away. Many people do not consider this an option because their pets are part of the family. In this case, the owners can take other steps to reduce pet allergens in the home. Keep the pet outside if possible, or at least train it to stay off frequently used chairs or sofas. Giving pets a bath every week or wiping them with special solutions designed to clean fur and skin may reduce dander. A nonallergic member of the family should brush the pet weekly, preferably outdoors, and should be the one to empty the cat-litter box. Cats and dogs are not the only allergy-producing pets. Birds and rodents, such as rabbits and guinea pigs, may also cause allergies.

Hardwood, tile, or linoleum floors are better than carpets, which can be dust traps. If it is not possible to remove carpets and rugs, then they should be vacuumed every few days. Conventional vacuum cleaners can actually stir up more dust in the air, but there are special anti-allergy vacuum cleaners that do a better job of trapping tiny allergens. The best have a high-efficiency particulate arresting (HEPA) filter. Chemicals that break down the dust mite allergens or kill the dust mites themselves can be sprayed on the carpets.

Avoid using heavy drapes and venetian blinds, or have them cleaned frequently. Window shades or washable curtains are easier to keep clean. Reduce the number of stuffed animals and knickknacks.

Dust mites and mold both thrive in humid places. Central air-conditioning is the best way of controlling humidity in the summer. Dehumidifiers can be used in the winter, especially in the basement, but it is important to clean them every day. Otherwise, mold can grow in the tank, making problems even worse. Air-filtering devices can remove airborne allergens, too,

The North American house dust mite, greatly magnified in this photograph, is too tiny to see with the naked eye. Dust mites can cause allergic reactions in susceptible people.

but some types may produce ozone. Ozone can irritate the nose and airways of people with allergies and asthma.

Irritating chemicals often found in buildings can worsen allergies, especially asthma. Tobacco smoke—firsthand or sec-ondhand—is one of the worst offenders. Others include perfumes, incense, cleaning products, paint, floor wax, and smoke from wood stoves or fireplaces.

Avoiding Outdoor Allergens

Central air-conditioning does a good job of keeping tree, grass, and weed pollens out of the house, but who wants to spend the entire summer inside? For years, people with allergies moved to desert locales to escape pollens, but they soon found that native desert plants also produce allergenic pollens. In addition, many of these new residents could not resist planting the familiar grassy lawns and gardens, complete with pollen-producing shade trees. As a result, Tucson, Arizona, now has the fastest-growing pollen count in the country.[3] Remember that ragweed pollen can be carried by wind currents for hundreds of miles. The only parts of the United States nearly free of ragweed are the Pacific Coast, the southern tip of Florida, and northwest Maine.[4]

Fortunately, there are other, less drastic measures that people with seasonal allergies can take to minimize exposure to outdoor allergens. Some radio stations and newspapers announce or publish daily pollen counts. While these numbers may be useful as a general guide, they are not very reliable. The amount of pollen in the air can vary between downtown and residential areas, and from one hour to another.[5] It is better to follow some basic practices. Avoid outdoor activities when pollen counts are highest: in the morning from 5 to 10 A.M. Dry, windy days really stir the pollen up; pollen counts are lowest on cool, moist days (on the other hand, these are ideal conditions for molds). Harvesttime is often high-pollen time in the country. If possible, plan to stay inside an air-conditioned building or car during these times.

Lawns should be kept closely trimmed; for many people, there is nothing worse than a lawn with grass that is producing seed. If at all possible, the allergy sufferer should get someone else to mow the lawn and rake the leaves. Otherwise, a tight-fitting dust mask can filter out some pollens. Gardeners can plant flowers, shrubs, and trees that are pollinated by insects, not the wind. At the end of a pollen-heavy day outside, a good shower, hair washing, and a change into clean clothes can help keep pollens out of the bedroom and, most important, off the pillow.

If all else fails, consider taking a vacation to a more pollen-free spot during the height of the pollen season. The seashore is a good bet.

Grass surrounding the home of an allergy sufferer should be kept trimmed because pollen from the grass seed can make allergies flare up.

Away, You Pesky Bugs!

Everyone would like to avoid insect stings, of course, but people who are allergic to insect venom need to take extra precautions. When working outside, wear long-sleeved shirts, long pants, gloves, and shoes. Do not wear brightly colored or pastel clothing, scented cosmetics, perfumes, or hair spray—they all attract insects. Take care when cooking or eating outdoors: Yellow jackets often decide to join the feast.

Be aware of insect nests. None of the stinging insects take kindly to having their homes disturbed. Honeybees live not only in hives but in trees as well. Yellow jackets often build their nests in the ground, under stones, and against the walls of buildings. It is common to stir up a yellow jacket nest when mowing the lawn or gardening. Hornets and wasps build their nests on tree branches or under the eaves of houses. Stinging fire ants build large, distinctive mounds. Take care when painting the house, putting up storm windows, or cleaning the gutters.

Insect nests near the home of an allergic person should be removed or destroyed—by someone who is not allergic to insect venom! Professional exterminators may be required to deal with hard-to-reach nests, especially those of hornets and wasps, which can be aggressive. Otherwise, a nest can be removed with a stick or stream of water, then placed immediately into a sealed container and discarded. Yellow jacket nests are best dealt with by pouring gasoline, kerosene, or lye into the entrance of the nest, in the evening when all the residents are at home. Do not set the nest afire; the fumes from the chemicals themselves kill the insects. A local beekeeper looking for more bees may be glad to help remove a beehive.

Anyone who is allergic to insect stings should learn to use, and carry with them, an emergency kit containing epinephrine (adrenaline), which counteracts anaphylactic shock. Epinephrine is available only through a doctor's prescription.

Touch Me Not!

"Leaves of three, let it be; leaves of five, let it thrive." This familiar adage has helped countless people distinguish the three-leafed poison ivy vine from the five-leafed Virginia creeper, a harmless vine. Those who live in areas where poison ivy, poison oak, or poison sumac grow should learn to recognize these plants. It is best to avoid them altogether, of course, but there are nonprescription creams that, when applied to the skin before exposure to the plants, will considerably reduce the severity of the reaction. Getting rid of poison ivy plants is not for the weakhearted: Wear shoes, a long-sleeved shirt, long pants, and gloves when pulling them up. The plants themselves should be buried, not burned, because the smoke carries dangerous fumes. After the cleanup, wash all clothes, shoes, gloves, tools—anything that might have touched the poisonous plants. Other plants, including heliotrope, ragweed, chrysanthemums, sagebrush, limes, oranges, celery, daisies, and potatoes, can also cause contact dermatitis.

Those who are allergic to skin-care or beauty products should try using hypoallergenic ones, which contain only substances unlikely to cause allergies. Many products on the shelf claim to be hypoallergenic, but in many cases it is just a marketing ploy. A list of companies that make truly hypoallergenic products is available from the Asthma and Allergy Foundation of America. Sometimes, avoiding contact dermatitis is as easy as switching perfumes or shampoos: An allergen may well be present in one product but not in another.

It is more difficult to avoid exposure to latex. Some health care professionals, like Lieutenant Harold Henderson, a Navy emergency nurse, have had to give up their jobs altogether. Henderson and others have become so sensitized to latex proteins that even breathing the air in the same room where someone else has removed latex gloves can set off a potentially fatal reaction. "I have to watch, for the rest of my life, every single thing I come in contact with," says Henderson.[6] Experts recommend that patients allergic to latex proteins carry nonlatex (vinyl) gloves with them at all times for health professionals to use during routine examinations and emergency procedures; wear a Medic Alert bracelet; and carry an emergency epinephrine kit. Although many common items—bras, underwear, and socks, for example—may contain latex, there are alternatives that use synthetic rubber instead. The manufacturer can provide this information.

Preventing Food Allergies

The only way of preventing food allergies is to avoid the offending allergens altogether. Unfortunately, the most

Peanuts are one of the most common food allergens.

common food allergens—milk, eggs, wheat, peanut and soy products, tree nuts, fish, and shellfish—are seemingly everywhere. Those who have food allergies—or their parents—must learn to read food labels carefully and ask waiters in restaurants to double-check ingredients and food preparation methods with the chef.[7] When eating at the home of friends, make sure they are aware of your food allergies ahead of time, and remind them that you cannot have "even a little bit."

Susan Carlton, a writer, has a daughter who is allergic to milk and eggs. "The first time I went grocery shopping after Jane's diagnosis," she writes, "I spent nearly an hour in the bread aisle trying to find a single loaf of whole-wheat bread made without milk."[8] Milk comes in many forms, she learned: whey, casein, lactalbumin, lactoglobulin. Eggs appear as ovomucin, albumin, vitellin, ovoglobulin, and livetin. Both turn up in the most unexpected places, including spaghetti sauce and wheat crackers.

People with severe food allergies, especially if they also have asthma, should know how to use an emergency epinephrine kit and always keep one with them. They should also wear a Medic Alert bracelet. Just one mistake or one mislabeled food could be deadly.

Preventing Allergies Before They Start

There is some evidence that allergies can be reduced or prevented altogether, even in children at high risk for developing allergies (that is, either both parents have allergies, or one parent and one sibling have allergies). Early exposure to allergens, before the immune system is fully developed, may trigger allergies in at-risk babies. For this reason, parents should delay giving allergenic foods—cow's milk, wheat, soy, corn, citrus, eggs, peanuts, and fish—to these children until they are a year old. Then, let the baby try them cautiously, one at a time. Breast-feeding the baby, even for as little as four to six months, may help prevent the development of eczema, as well as food and respiratory allergies.[9] Because small amounts of allergens can enter the mother's breast milk, the breast-feeding mother should also try to avoid allergenic foods as much as possible.

The development of asthma and allergies to dust mites in later childhood is directly related to exposure to dust mites in early infancy.[10] Scientists have shown that infants exposed to cats from birth are more likely to develop allergies to cat dander later on.[11] A child at risk for developing allergies may benefit from avoiding these allergens early in life.

Parents who smoke would be wise to stop—not just for their own health, but for their children's health as well. Mothers who smoke cigarettes (or who breathe a lot of someone else's tobacco smoke) while pregnant, and when their children are young, put their children at greater risk for developing asthma.[12] There is some evidence that mothers who smoke while pregnant may put their children at greater risk for developing eczema as well.[13]

Although limiting a baby's exposure to potential allergens can be a difficult task for parents, the benefits are great for children who are at high risk for developing allergies. In one study, parents who followed a strict plan to avoid exposing their at-risk babies to food and dust mite allergens for the first year of life were compared with a similar group who followed no special plan. At age four, the children with limited exposure to allergens as babies had significantly fewer allergies than the children in the control group.[14]

6
Treating Allergies

Seven-year-old Katie DeWitt was excited about attending a birthday party at the home of her friends, twins Alison and Caitlin. They played party games, romped with the three cats that lived in the house, ate birthday cake, and opened presents. But it was not long before Katie's fun turned into misery. Her eyes itched and watered, she sneezed and sniffled almost constantly, and it was hard for her to breathe. By the end of the party, she was a wreck. Katie was allergic to cats—much more than either of her parents suspected. Even so, Katie attended Caitlin and Alison's next birthday party, and without any noticeable symptoms. Her secret? Before going to the party, she had taken an antihistamine, a medicine that blocks the action of histamine. "Avoidance is the best medicine," says Katie's mother, "but sometimes that's not possible. An advance dose of antihistamine can really work wonders."[1]

Katie is in good company: Millions of other Americans turn to medicines when their allergies flare up—or threaten to. Although antihistamines remain the most commonly used allergy medication, a wide variety of medical options is available to the allergy sufferer.

Medicines for Allergic Rhinitis

Antihistamines are the drug of choice for people whose allergies are relatively mild or surface only occasionally. Recall (Chapter 3) that IgE-related allergies are caused by the release of histamine, which binds to certain cell receptors. This causes small blood vessels to swell and become leaky and irritates nerve endings, resulting in an itchy feeling. It may cause the muscles around the bronchial tubes to swell. Because antihistamine molecules are shaped somewhat like histamine molecules, they can also bind to histamine receptors on cells. Unlike histamine, however, antihistamines have no other effect on the cells. If an antihistamine drug is taken *before* histamine is released—and symptoms begin—the histamine molecules end up losers in the game of musical receptors. This is why it is most effective to take a preventive dose of antihistamine.

Over-the-counter antihistamines are inexpensive and provide allergy relief within fifteen to twenty minutes. Unfortunately, they can also cause drowsiness—a welcome effect at night, but not during the day. Some of the newer antihistamines, currently available by prescription only, do not cause drowsiness. They are effective, but more expensive than

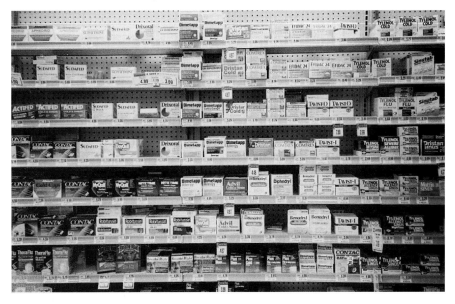

Many over-the-counter allergy and cold medicines are available at the pharmacy.

the older antihistamines, and may have serious side effects in some people. Some unlucky people are allergic to antihistamines themselves.

Antihistamines are often used along with decongestants, which constrict blood vessels. Although nasal spray decongestants are faster acting and more effective than the pill form, they should not be used for more than three to five days. If used longer, they can cause "rebound" congestion, making it necessary to take more and more decongestant.

A drug called cromolyn sodium, available as a nasal spray or as eyedrops, may relieve IgE-related allergy symptoms in some people. It acts on the mast cells, reducing the amount of histamine released. Cromolyn sodium does not work for everyone (and people who wear contact lenses should not use the eyedrops at all). The drug must be taken four times a day, starting a few weeks before allergy season. But because there are virtually no side effects, many allergists believe it is worth a try. It is now available without a doctor's prescription.

Prescription-only nasal sprays with corticosteroids (unrelated to the anabolic steroids misused by some athletes) can be very effective in preventing the nasal symptoms of hay fever. They work by reducing inflammation in the nasal passages. They appear to be safe for long-term use and have few side effects. Like cromolyn sodium, there is no immediate response. They can take up to two weeks to work.

Although many allergy medicines are available over-the-counter, they, like all drugs, should be used with caution. Read the labels carefully. Ask your pharmacist to tell you about the proper use of allergy medicines. People with severe allergies or other important medical conditions (such as kidney, liver, or heart disease) should consult a doctor before using allergy medications. A qualified physician can help you choose a treatment best suited for your needs, and can alert you to possible side effects.

Medicines for Asthma

Until fairly recently, the mainstay of asthma therapy had been medicines that quickly relax tight airway muscles, making it easier to breathe in the event of an asthma attack. Called bronchodilators, these medicines are inhaled, usually through a handheld device called an inhaler. They continue to be, as one leading allergist puts it, "wonderful drugs, which provide quick, effective relief for most individuals, usually within about fifteen minutes and lasting for four to six hours."[2]

Yet there is a danger in relying too heavily on bronchodilators, something many people are inclined to do. Bronchodilators do not treat the underlying inflammation. In fact, by allowing the asthmatic to breathe in even more allergens, bronchodilators may worsen inflammation. For this reason, it is important not to use bronchodilators more frequently than recommended. Asthmatics who need to use their bronchodilators more often than three or four times a day should consult their doctors; additional medication may be needed to control the disease.

Most physicians now agree that long-term preventive medications are necessary for all but the mildest forms of asthma. Anti-inflammatory drugs—usually delivered by inhalers—are the current mainstay of asthma therapy. Cromolyn sodium may work for some people, especially those with mild cases of asthma. Corticosteroids are the most effective anti-inflammatory agents and, when they are inhaled in low doses, are considered safe for long-term use, even in children. Doctors may prescribe oral corticosteroids for people with severe asthma, but because they may have serious side effects, they are not recommended for long-term use.

Doctors may also prescribe a long-acting bronchodilator such as theophylline to help relax airways and make breathing easier. They advise asthmatics to take these, and the anti-inflammatory drugs previously described, on a regular schedule.

Severe asthma attacks, if not helped by a bronchodilator, may require an immediate injection of epinephrine (adrenaline) or corticosteroids. Doctors often advise those with severe asthma to learn how to give themselves an injection of epinephrine in the event of a major asthma attack.[3]

Like diabetes, asthma is a chronic disease—it can be controlled, but not cured. Asthmatics can estimate the amount of air they can blow out of their lungs by blowing into a device called a peak flow meter. Regular monitoring allows asthmatics to detect changes in their lung function *before* a crisis occurs. They can adjust their activities or medications accordingly. Even if asthma seems to be under control, asthmatics should not stop taking their medications without first consulting their doctor.

If you think you have asthma, it is important to see a doctor and take the medications as prescribed. Do not take over-the-counter medications for asthma without consulting a doctor first. They can speed up the heart rate, sometimes dangerously so. And by temporarily masking the severity of the disease, they can give a false sense of security.

Treatment for Eczema and Contact Dermatitis

Aside from avoiding the allergens that cause eczema and contact dermatitis, therapy for these diseases generally consists of relieving the symptoms. If you know you have brushed up against poison ivy, wash the affected area as soon as possible with cool water (do not use soap; it can spread the toxic oils) followed by rubbing alcohol. Very mild eczema and contact dermatitis rashes can be treated with over-the-counter cortisone creams, but if the rash lasts longer than one or two weeks, consult a doctor. More severe rashes often require a prescription-strength steroid cream or ointment to help reduce inflammation. The doctor may also prescribe antihistamines to help reduce the all-over itchy feeling of eczema.

People with eczema often have very dry skin, so many doctors recommend a warm bath two to three times a day, followed by a good moisturizing lotion. Because it is so tempting to scratch an eczema rash, sometimes people take special measures to prevent scratching, such as covering the affected areas with bandages or trimming fingernails. Sometimes it is necessary to use mittens or restraints to prevent an infant from scratching.[4]

Treatment for Anaphylaxis

Dr. Stephen Kemp, a thirty-four-year-old allergist and immunologist, knew that he was asthmatic and allergic to peanuts, almonds, and pecans. So when he ate some commercially made gingersnap cookies, he did not worry because the package label did not list peanuts among the ingredients. But within five minutes, the roof of his mouth began to itch, he had difficulty breathing and swallowing, stomach cramps, a stuffy nose, and itchy, watery eyes. His heart raced and he felt light-headed. He knew that he was having an anaphylactic reaction. He gave himself a shot of epinephrine to stop the release of histamine and other chemical mediators of the allergic reaction. This bought him enough time to get to the emergency room, where the medical staff gave him additional drugs to help stabilize his condition.

Tests revealed that there were indeed trace amounts of peanut allergen in the cookies Kemp ate—possibly resulting from accidental contamination at the cookie factory.[5]

The treatments for anaphylaxis are simple: avoidance and emergency measures. Unfortunately, as Kemp's experience shows, sometimes even those most knowledgeable about their disease can encounter allergens unexpectedly. Anyone who has had an anaphylactic reaction in the past, or is allergic to insect stings, certain foods, or latex proteins, should have on hand and know how to use emergency epinephrine.

One easy-to-use device is the EpiPen® (or the EpiPen Jr.® for children), which looks like a large ballpoint pen. It delivers a pre-measured dose of epinephrine when it is pressed against the skin surface, usually on the thigh. Some doctors may recommend the Ana-Kit®, which contains a syringe, needle, two doses of epinephrine, and antihistamine tablets. Both the EpiPen® and the Ana-Kit® are available only by a doctor's prescription. Meanwhile, the patient should be rushed to the emergency room, even if the reaction appears to be under control: There may be a late-phase reaction that requires additional treatment.[6]

Anyone who has had an anaphylactic reaction should wear a Medic Alert identification tag or bracelet, giving information about the nature of the allergy and the treatment for a reaction.

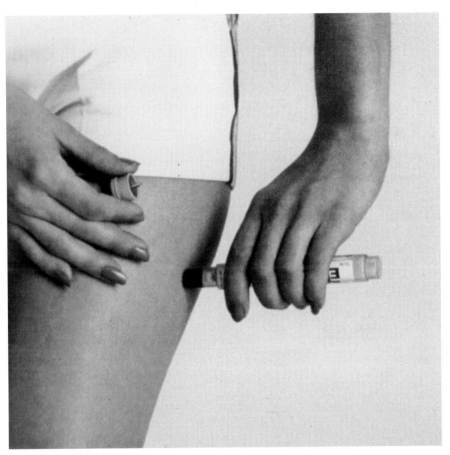

When pressed against the skin, the EpiPen® sends epinephrine into the body. It can be used for anaphylactic reactions to insect stings, foods, and drugs.

Immunotherapy (Allergy Shots)

Some people are not helped by allergy drugs, or cannot tolerate them. Those with insect venom allergies have no non-emergency drugs to turn to. These people might be good candidates for allergy shots, or allergen immunotherapy. This is a treatment in which people with allergies receive regular doses of purified allergen over a period of time, in order to decrease the immune system's sensitivity to that allergen. They are very effective and highly recommended for people with allergies to insect venom. Most people with allergies to dust mites, cat dander, and tree, grass, or weed pollens benefit from immunotherapy.[7]

While some people have great success with allergy shots, they are not a quick fix: They require a long-term commitment of time and money. A typical three-year course of allergy shots at a midwestern clinic, for example, will cost about $2,000, not including the cost of the initial diagnosis.[8] And they are not usually effective or recommended for people with eczema or food, drug, or chemical allergies. Their use in the treatment of asthma is controversial, although there is some evidence that they might help asthmatics with allergies to dust mites, pollens, and cats.[9]

The treatment begins with shots, just under the skin, of very dilute allergen extracts, once or twice a week. Every week, the dose is gradually increased, until a maintenance dose is reached—usually after about six months. After that, the shots are usually given once a month, generally for three to five years. Most people who benefit from allergy shots will see some improvement within a year after reaching the maintenance dose. Some may benefit from allergy shots after only a few months.

Immunotherapy is not without its risks. Because it involves injecting purified allergen, there is always a slight chance that the patient will have an anaphylactic reaction. (A little redness, itching, or swelling around the site of injection is common and not a cause for worry; these symptoms can be helped by antihistamines, cold compresses, or corticosteroid creams.) The chance that anaphylaxis can occur is the reason why allergy shots must always be given in a doctor's office, with emergency epinephrine on hand. Because most severe reactions occur within thirty minutes of the injection, the American Academy of Allergy, Asthma and Immunology recommends that patients remain in the doctor's office for that time.[10]

How Do Allergy Shots Work?

Scientists are not sure why immunotherapy works. The prevailing theory is that very small doses of allergen promote the production of a blocking antibody—an IgG antibody that recognizes the allergen and prevents it from interacting with IgE antibodies on mast cells. It also seems to suppress further production of IgE antibodies and alters the kinds of chemical messengers produced by T cells.[11]

7

The High Cost of Allergies

Mike Ivy attended college on an academic scholarship, played varsity football, held down a job, and helped raise his two-year-old daughter. Although asthma had been his companion since the age of eleven, he had never let it slow him down. But one evening, he had an asthma attack that sent him, gasping for air, to the emergency room. Less than an hour and a half later, Mike Ivy was pronounced dead. He was twenty years old.[1]

Mike is part of a disturbing national trend: Among young people, the rate of reported deaths from asthma more than doubled between 1980 and 1993. Especially hard hit were people like Mike: young African Americans. In 1993, among fifteen- to twenty- year-olds, blacks were six times more likely than whites to die of asthma. More and more young people are being hospitalized for asthma.[2]

"There's no reasonable justification for the growing number of asthma deaths among children and young adults in this country," says Ira Finegold, M.D., president of the American College of Allergy, Asthma and Immunology. "Asthma is a disease we know how to control."[3]

The death of Mike Ivy and others like him shows how important it is for asthmatics and allergy sufferers to understand their conditions early in life. They must learn to recognize the allergens that make them sick, and avoid them when possible. When an allergy or asthma attack does occur, they should recognize their symptoms and treat them according to their doctor's instructions.

Most people are not at risk of dying from asthma or other allergies. Even so, allergic reactions often interfere with work, school, or play. It is hard to concentrate when you're constantly sneezing, sniffling, and wiping your watery eyes! Feeling good about the way you look is difficult if your arms are covered with an itchy red rash. And most allergy sufferers say that people who do not have allergies do not really understand the extent of their misery.[4] Parents of children with asthma say that teachers at school may think their children are faking breathing problems, or that the disease is "all in their heads."[5]

This belief probably stems from an old theory—long disproved—that asthma is caused by an anxious mother or a nervous child's overactive imagination. While it is true that psychological factors, especially stress, may worsen asthma, eczema, and hives, they are not the cause. On the other hand,

85

Allergies, such as hay fever, can interfere with a person's outdoor activities.

the stress of living with allergies—missed days from school or work, increased medical costs, and limits on physical activity—can cause emotional problems.[6]

In addition, allergy medicines may have an effect on behavior. Many antihistamines, for example, make people feel sleepy (although there may be an opposite effect on some people, especially children). Some of the medicines used to treat asthma may cause restlessness, anxiety, or difficulty in concentrating. The long-term use of corticosteroids can also cause mood swings.

If you feel that allergy medicine or the disease itself is causing anxiety, stress, or moodiness, it is a good idea to tell your doctor. He or she should be sympathetic, and may recommend psychological counseling. Some allergy patients find the relaxation and breathing exercises taught in yoga classes to be helpful.

There are enormous financial costs to allergies. Americans spend a lot of money trying to keep their allergies and asthma under control—more than one billion dollars each year for visits to the doctor and over-the-counter and prescription medicines. Society pays, too. About 4 million workdays are lost each year due to hay fever alone.[7] Every year, allergies cost workers $200 million in lost wages and employers $639 million in lost productivity.[8]

Work-related allergies are common. Veterinarians and others who work with animals often develop allergies to animal dander, saliva, or urine. Hairdressers may develop allergic rashes in response to hair dyes or other chemicals.

Some work-related allergies are so common that they have names of their own: cheese-worker's lung, malt-worker's disease, baker's asthma.

Sue Lockwood, a surgical technician, has developed an allergy to latex proteins. She is so sensitive that even if she were to wear allergen-free vinyl gloves during surgery, just breathing latex particles from the rest of the surgery team's gloves would cause her problems. "There's no way I can work in surgery anymore," she says. "I want my career back."[9]

Ideally, those who develop work-related allergies should get medical help and tell their employers. It may be possible to avoid allergic reactions by improving working conditions or wearing a face mask. If those measures do not work, the employer may offer retraining for a new job.

It is clear that allergies cause a great deal of misery. What's more, they cost the nation billions of dollars each year. Most allergy treatments focus on the symptoms, but researchers are working on ways to stop the allergic reaction before it starts.

Why Is Asthma on the Rise?

There is some evidence that the rise in asthma and other allergic diseases may actually be related to a decline in childhood infections. One recent study has shown that schoolchildren in Japan who had been infected with the bacteria that cause tuberculosis (TB) were much less likely to have allergies than children who had never been exposed to the bacteria. The scientists suggest that early childhood infections may prod the immune system to make fewer of the allergy-related TH2 cells.[10]

Changes in our environment have almost certainly contributed to the increase in asthma-related hospitalizations and deaths. Today's airtight homes and offices are traps for indoor allergens and pollutants, especially tobacco smoke. Inner cities are plagued by air pollution. These irritants all make asthma worse.

One of the major reasons that asthma has become such a serious problem has nothing to do with science or medicine. A growing number of people have poor access to health care. Those who cannot afford health insurance are sometimes forced to wait until there is an emergency before going to the doctor. Family and school problems may make asthma symptoms worse. "It's essential that children with asthma have access to the kinds of medical specialists who understand the disease and can help them control it," said Dr. Finegold.[11]

8

The Future of
Allergy Research

Everyone, it seems, either suffers from allergies or knows someone who does. One might think that scientists must know a great deal about such a common disease. Yet in many respects, allergies are still a mystery. Why do some people seem to have allergies to everything under the sun, while others breeze through life unconcerned by pollen, dust, or cats? Why do some people have mild allergies, while others know they may die from an allergic reaction? Why do we have IgE antibodies at all? Researchers are just beginning to answer some of these basic questions about allergies. They hope that the answers will lead to better allergy medicines—drugs that stop the allergic process before it starts. This chapter is a sampling of what is "hot" in allergy research today.

Stopping Allergies in Their Tracks

If you were to develop a drug to stop allergies, where would you begin? One way would be to prevent IgE antibodies from binding to mast cells in the first place. That is the approach two research companies—Tanox, in Houston, Texas (in partnership with Novardis), and Genentech, in San Francisco, California—decided to take. They isolated IgE antibodies from people, and injected these antibodies into mice. The mouse B cells, recognizing the human IgE antibodies as foreign, began producing anti-IgE antibodies. Some of the anti-IgE antibodies specifically recognized the antibody's mast cell binding site. The scientists purified these B cells, made them immortal by fusing them with cancer cells, and grew them in culture. Now they had a steady supply of specific anti-IgE antibodies that could prevent IgE from binding to mast cells. To make these mouse antibodies look more like human antibodies, they used genetic engineering techniques to produce a chimeric antibody: one that was half mouse, half human (the Greeks coined the word *chimera* to describe a mythical beast having the body parts of several different animals).

The companies are currently testing the anti-IgE antibodies in humans, with promising early results. "With our antibody," says the Tanox vice-president for research and development, "the IgE in the blood disappears almost immediately."[1] The drawback: The anti-IgE antibodies must be injected weekly, possibly for life.

91

A team of scientists from Philadelphia and London has taken a slightly different approach: They have made two protein fragments (peptides) that mimic the binding portion of the mast cell's IgE receptor.[2] By binding to IgE before it even reaches mast cells, the peptides could prevent an allergic response. Do not expect to see a drug using this technology in your pharmacy anytime soon, though—the research is still in the early stages.

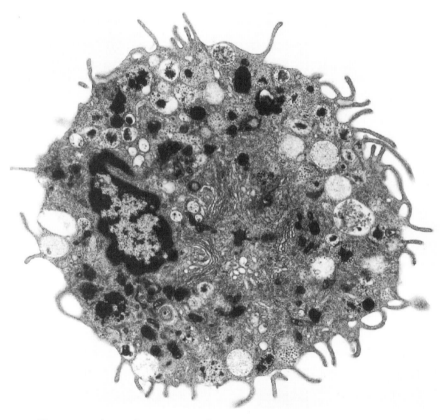

New research involving mast cells may prove successful in preventing allergic responses.

What if you could prevent B cells from producing IgE in the first place? Remember (Chapter 3) that B cells make IgE only after they have received the go-ahead signal, a protein called IL4, from TH2 cells. Researchers made a mutant IL4 protein that binds to the IL4 receptor on the B cell without prompting it to make IgE. No one has tried the mutant IL4 protein in humans yet, but early studies in mice look promising.[3]

How about shutting off IL4 production altogether? This approach came about from conventional allergen immunotherapy. With allergy shots, you will remember (Chapter 6), people are given gradually increasing doses of purified allergen over a period of time. When the shots work, people eventually lose their sensitivity to allergens. Their T cells stop producing IL4 and instruct B cells to produce harmless IgG antibody instead.

But allergy shots are not always effective. And injecting someone with a known allergen always carries with it the risk of IgE-induced side effects—including a life-threatening anaphylactic reaction. For this reason, doctors begin a course of allergy shots with very small doses of allergen, slowly increasing to a maximum level. It is a long, expensive process.

Researchers at the ImmunLogic Pharmaceutical Corporation in Waltham, Massachusetts, have found a way to make allergen-specific T cells less sensitive. They inject the patient with pieces of the allergen, called peptides. These peptides bind very strongly to T cell receptors, but not to IgE antibodies. When given in high enough doses, they can "turn off" the peptide-specific T cells. These T cells are unable to produce IL4 when the real allergen comes along, so they do not instruct B cells to produce IgE antibody. Best of all, the injections are given over a course of weeks, not years.

ImmunLogic, in collaboration with scientists at the Johns Hopkins University Asthma and Allergy Center and the New England Medical Center in Boston, Massachusetts, is testing its cat dander peptide vaccine in people. In a preliminary study, the researchers found that people with cat allergies who received four injections of the vaccine during one month had significantly less sneezing, itching, watery eyes, and inflammation when they were around cats.[4] They will need to carry out further studies to determine how long the vaccine's effects last and how often follow-up injections are needed. If all goes well, according to one of the scientists, the cat peptide vaccine may be in the allergy clinics in a few years. ImmunLogic, along with another company, Hoechst Marion Roussel, is also developing other peptide-based vaccines—for ragweed, house-dust mites, Japanese cedar pollen, and grass.[5]

Researchers from Taiwan and the Johns Hopkins University School of Medicine in Baltimore, Maryland, are exploring a new twist on allergy shots. Instead of injecting the allergen or pieces of the allergen into their subjects, they inject deoxyribonucleic acid (DNA) containing the allergen genes instead. When they injected allergy-prone rats with dust mite allergen (Der p V) DNA, the rat muscle cells took up the DNA. The rat muscle cells used their own cell machinery to make Der p V. When this happened, the cell put the Der p V protein on its cell surface, where it remained for as long as six months. It worked! The rats who received the Der p V DNA made much less IgE antibody, and their cells released less histamine, when they were exposed to dust mite allergen. The scientists believe that a subset of T cells turned off IgE production, either by sending signals to the B cells or the TH2 cells.[6]

The allergen DNA vaccine has not been tried in humans yet. There are still a lot of unanswered questions: Could the allergen DNA insert itself into the host genome and disrupt normal cell function? What if the body decided to mount an all-out attack on the cells expressing the allergen? But many scientists believe this is a promising area of research.

New Hope for Food Allergies

The only effective treatment for food allergies today is avoiding the food that causes the problem. But scientists at the Johns Hopkins University School of Medicine are focusing on the peanut allergens (proteins) that cause allergic reactions, with expectations of developing more effective treatments for peanut allergies. In the process of identifying the allergens, the group has determined the building blocks—amino acids—in each protein, and the sequence in which they occur. Using this information, they can make new peanut proteins almost identical to the original ones. And by strategically changing just one amino acid, they can make it impossible for IgE antibodies to bind to the protein. "That protein would no longer be able to generate an allergic response, but it would still have all the T cell binding sites," says Johns Hopkins professor Hugh Sampson. Sampson and his group believe the modified allergen might be used to desensitize allergen-specific T cells. And, since they already know the DNA sequence for each allergen, they are also experimenting with peanut allergen DNA vaccines. "When we come up with a successful treatment strategy, it can be adapted to other food allergies," says Sampson. "This is a nice model for treatment of food allergy."[7]

The Genetics of Allergies

Who gets allergies, and how severely? Researchers are beginning to answer these questions by focusing on the genes that determine whether we have allergies. As might be expected of such a complex disease, there appear to be several genes that contribute to allergies.

William O. C. M. Cookson, in Oxford, England, and his colleagues have identified a gene that makes people especially prone to developing allergies. This gene is inherited only from the mother.[8] The group found that some families with allergies carry a variant of the gene, which codes for the IgE receptor carried on mast cells. "We think people who have this variant have a more sensitive [mast cell] trigger," says Cookson.[9]

Another group, led by David G. Marsh at the Johns Hopkins University School of Medicine, has found a region on a different chromosome that seems to control total IgE levels. This region contains, among other things, the gene coding for IL4. Marsh and his colleagues believe that one or more variations in the IL4 gene, or in a gene that controls the production of IL4, may result in higher-than-normal IL4 levels in the bloodstream. This might lead to unusually high levels of IgE in the bloodstream. Marsh notes that people with asthma, even those with no detectable allergies, have high IgE levels.[10]

Among people with allergies, about half experience what scientists call "late-phase response" six to twenty-four hours after exposure to the allergen, often long after the allergen has been cleared from the body. Mast cells recruit other immune cells, including basophils and eosinophils, to the scene of the allergic reaction. Basophils, which, like mast cells, carry IgE on their surface, release a host of chemicals, including histamine and IL4. Eosinophils release toxic proteins, which can damage local cells.

There is a whole family of proteins, called histamine-releasing factors (HRFs), that scientists believe are important in the late-phase response. HRFs cause other cells to release histamine, but some also help attract other immune cells. Susan MacDonald and her colleagues at the Johns Hopkins Asthma and Allergy Center have identified and described an HRF that depends on IgE bound to basophils.[11] This HRF ultimately causes B cells to switch from IgG to IgE production. She and her senior research associate, Jacqueline Langdon, spent years purifying the molecule, normally present in tiny quantities in the human body. Now MacDonald is busy looking for the HRF receptor. Once she has found a receptor, it might be possible to develop a drug that blocks the reaction.

Curiously, MacDonald found that only half of the people with allergies she tested had basophils that responded to HRFs—and that these people produced a special kind of IgE antibody (IgE+). MacDonald and other scientists suspect that people with high levels of the IgE+ antibody may have worse chronic allergies.

For now, allergy sufferers continue to sneeze, sniffle, and itch, helped—but usually not cured—by currently available drugs and therapies. But recent advances in immunology research in general, and allergy research in particular, are leading us to better ways of treating and even preventing allergies.

Q & A

Q. My mother is allergic to grass pollen, but I am allergic to cats and dust. If allergies are inherited, why aren't we allergic to the same things?

A. It is true that we inherit the tendency to be allergic, but we do not inherit a specific allergy. Exposure to allergens at a particular time—during infancy, after a viral infection, or during puberty, for example—may contribute to the development of specific allergies.

Q. When I drink milk, I feel bloated and get stomach cramps. Am I allergic to milk?

A. Not necessarily. You may be lactose intolerant instead. A person with lactose intolerance lacks an enzyme necessary for digesting milk sugar. A person with a food intolerance can often eat small amounts of the offending food without getting sick. Someone with a food allergy, however, should never eat even small amounts of the offending food. A food allergy occurs when the immune system reacts to a certain food. If you suspect you have a food allergy, check with an allergist.

Q. I want a cat, but I am allergic to my best friend's Persian. Should I get a short-haired cat instead?

A. The length of a cat's fur will not make any difference. You are allergic to cat dander, and maybe proteins in the saliva and urine. Consider fish or reptiles instead.

Q. My doctor says I have asthma. Does this mean I cannot exercise?

A. No. In fact, there are many athletes who have asthma. You may need to take special care when it is cold outside or during the pollen season. Ask your doctor how you can exercise safely.

Q. My aunt says that my asthma is "all in my head." Is she right?

A. No. Asthma is a potentially serious disease, caused by chronic inflammation in the airways. The airways of people with asthma are overly sensitive to environmental changes. Psychological stress can make asthma worse, but it does not cause asthma.

Q. I had a severe allergic reaction to a yellow jacket sting last year at a picnic. Now I am afraid to go on picnics. Any ideas?

A. There are several things you can do to avoid insect stings and still enjoy warm-weather activities. Do not wear bright clothing or fragrances or go barefoot outside during the summer. Try to avoid outdoor trash cans, which may attract insects, especially if they are uncovered. Make a special effort to keep away from insects in the early fall, when they become more aggressive and are more likely to sting. Wear a MedicAlert bracelet, and make sure you have a dose of epinephrine handy.

Q. My doctor says I am allergic to my favorite perfume! Does this mean I can never wear it again?

A. Once you develop an allergy to a particular substance, it is usually permanent. You are probably allergic to just one of the ingredients in the perfume. If you experiment with different perfumes, you may find a similar fragrance that lacks the allergenic substance.

Q. I often feel left out because I am allergic to a lot of things like grass pollens and cat dander. Where can I talk to others who have the same problems I do?

A. There are several support groups for people with allergies. You can find them by contacting the associations listed in this book (see "For More Information"). There are also special Internet mailing lists for people with allergies.

Q. Are people with allergies more likely to get ear infections?

A. Yes, they are. The ear is connected to the back of the nose through the eustachian tube. Fluid from the inner ear drains into the eustachian tube. When the nasal passages are inflamed and swollen from allergies, the eustachian tube can also become swollen and blocked. When fluid builds up in the inner ear, it can become infected, especially after a bacterial or viral infection.

Q. I'm allergic to peanuts, but I love peanut butter. Can I have just a little once in a while?

A. No, you cannot. As little as one half of a peanut has been known to cause a fatal reaction in severely allergic individuals. Even being kissed by someone who has eaten peanuts can cause a reaction.

Allergies Timeline

1565—Leonardo Botallo, an Italian physician, describes several cases of allergies.

1656—Pierre Borel performs first skin test, to determine the source of an allergy.

1819—John Bostock writes the first complete description of hay fever.

1871—Charles Blackley shows that hay fever is caused by grass pollen.

1880s—Louis Pasteur conducts the first modern controlled experiments in immunology.

1890—Emil von Behring and Shibasaburo Kitasato discover antitoxin; Robert Koch discovers delayed-type hypersensitivity reaction.

1901—Paul Portier and Charles Richet describe anaphylaxis.

1906—Clemens von Pirquet and Béla Schick show that serum sickness is caused by the immune system; von Pirquet coins word *allergy*.

1910—Scientists show that hay fever and asthma are allergies; Sir Henry Dale isolates histamine.

1911—Leonard Noon develops allergy treatment later known as "allergy shots."

1921—Carl Prausnitz and Heinz Küstner discover passive transfer of allergy with serum.

1932—Wilhelm Feldberg and Carl Draystedt show that histamine is released in the anaphylactic reaction.

1937—Daniel Bovet develops antihistamine.

1966—Kimishige Ishizaka and Teruko Ishizaka discover IgE antibodies.

For More Information

Allergy and Asthma Network/
Mothers of Asthmatics, Inc.
3554 Chain Bridge Road, Suite 200
Fairfax, VA 22030
(800) 878-4403 or (703) 385-4403
http://www.podi.com/health/aanma/

American Academy of Allergy,
Asthma and Immunology
611 East Wells Street
Milwaukee, WI 53202
(800) 822-ASMA
http://www.aaaai.org/

American College of Allergy,
Asthma and Immunology
85 West Algonquin Road, Suite 550
Arlington Heights, IL 60005
(847) 427-1200
http://allergy.mcg.edu/

Asthma and Allergy Foundation of America
1125 15th Street, N.W., Suite 502
Washington, DC 20005
(800) 727-8462 or (202) 466-7643

The Food Allergy Network
10400 Eaton Place, Suite 107
Fairfax, VA 22030
(800) 929-4040 or (703) 691-2713
http://www.foodallergy.org/

**National Institute of Allergy
and Infectious Diseases
National Institutes of Health**
Bethesda, MD 20892
http://www.niaid.nih.gov/

Internet Sources

Allergy Internet Resources, a World Wide Web site containing a variety of links to allergy-related sites and an allergy discussion list.

http://www.io.com/allergy/allabc.html#top

The Asthma Information Center, sponsored by the Journal of the American Medical Association.

http://www.ama-assn.org/special/asthma/asthma.htm

Chapter Notes

Chapter 1. Allergies: They Are Nothing to Sneeze At

1. Bill Benner, "Amy Van Dyken Leads the Final-Day Charge by the U.S.," *The Indianapolis Star*, July 27, 1996, p. C1.

2. Bonnie DeSimone, "Coming Up Without Air," *Chicago Tribune*, July 1, 1996, Section 3, p. 1.

3. Ibid.

4. Lawrence M. Lichtenstein, "Allergy and the Immune System," *Scientific American*, September 1993, pp. 117–124.

5. Centers for Disease Control and Prevention (CDC), "Asthma Mortality and Hospitalization Among Children and Young Adults—United States, 1980–1993," *Morbidity and Mortality Weekly Report*, vol. 45, no. 17, May 3, 1996, p. 350.

6. Stuart H. Young, M.D., Bruce S. Dobozin, M.D., and Margaret Miner, *Allergies: The Complete Guide to Diagnosis, Treatment, and Daily Management* (Yonkers, N.Y.: Consumer Reports Books, 1991), pp. 88–89.

7. Geoffrey Cowley with Robina Riccitiello, "An End to the Misery?" *Newsweek*, December 26, 1994/January 2, 1995, pp. 116–117.

Chapter 2. How We Came to Understand Allergies

1. Titus Lucretius Carus, *De Rerum Natura (On the Nature of Things)*, trans. W.H.D. Rouse (Cambridge, Mass.: Harvard University Press [The Loeb Classical Library], 1966), Book IV, line 637.

2. Charles Singer and E. Ashworth Underwood, *A Short History of Medicine* (New York: Oxford University Press, 1962), p. 428.

3. Ibid., p. 427.

4. Maurice Lessof, "Allergy," in *The Oxford Medical Companion*, ed. John Walton, Jeremiah A. Barondess, and Stephen Lock (Oxford, Eng.: Oxford University Press, 1994), p. 20.

5. Ronald Finn, "John Bostock, Hay Fever, and the Mechanism of Allergy," *The Lancet,* vol. 340, December 12, 1992, pp. 1453–1455.

6. Ibid., p. 1454.

7. Charles D. May, M.D., "The Ancestry of Allergy: Being an Account of the Original Experimental Induction of Hypersensitivity Recognizing the Contribution of Paul Portier," *Journal of Allergy and Clinical Immunology*, 1985, vol. 75, no. 4, pp. 485–495.

8. Sheldon G. Cohen, M.D., and Max Samter, M.D., eds., Excerpts from *Classics in Immunology*, 2nd edition (Carlsbad, Calif.: Symposia Foundation, 1992), p. 5.

9. Arthur M. Silverstein, *A History of Immunology* (San Diego, Calif.: Academic Press, Inc., 1989), p. 214.

10. Deborah Bibel, ed., *Milestones in Immunology* (Madison, Wis.: Science Tech Publishers, 1988), p. 58.

11. Ibid., p. 47.

Chapter 3. What Are Allergies?

1. Susan Carlton, "Living with Food Allergies," *Parents,* August 1995, pp. 28–31.

2. Abe Brown, "All About Allergy and Asthma," *Current Health,* October 1993, pp. 6–11.

3. William Cookson, "The Genetics of Atopy," *Journal of Allergy and Clinical Immunology,* vol. 94, no. 3, part 2, September 1994, pp. 643–644.

4. Peter Radetsky, "Of Parasites and Pollen," *Discover,* September 1993, pp. 56–62.

5. William J. Davis, "Allergic Rhinitis—Pollen," in *The Columbia University College of Physicians & Surgeons Complete Home Medical Guide,* revised edition, ed. Donald F. Tapley, M.D., Thomas Q. Morris, M.D., Lewis P. Rowland, M.D., and Robert J. Weiss, M.D. (New York: Crown Publishers, Inc., 1989), p. 683.

6. A. M. Rees, ed., *Consumer Health USA* (Phoenix, Ariz.: Oryx Press, 1995), p. 18.

7. Michael Kaliner, M.D., and Robert Lemanske, M.D., "Rhinitis and Asthma," *Journal of the American Medical Association,* vol. 268, no. 20, November 25, 1992, p. 2815.

8. Stuart H. Young, M.D., Bruce S. Dobozin, M.D., Margaret Miner, and the editors of *Consumer Reports Books, Allergies: The Complete Guide to Diagnosis, Treatment, and Daily Management* (Yonkers, N.Y.: Consumer Reports Books, 1991), p. 185.

9. Martin D. Valentine, M.D., "Anaphylaxis and Stinging Insect Hypersensitivity," *Journal of the American Medical Association,* vol. 268, no. 20, November 25, 1992, p. 2831.

10. J. M. James, P. A. Eigenmann, P. A. Eggleston, and H. A. Sampson, "Airway Reactivity Changes in Asthmatic Patients Undergoing Blinded Food Challenges," *American Journal of Respiratory and Critical Care Medicine*, vol. 153, no. 2, February 1996, pp. 597–603.

11. Young, p. 99.

12. Janet Raloff, "Latex Allergies from Right Out of Thin Air?" *Science News*, vol. 147, no. 16, April 22, 1995, p. 244.

13. Lawrence P. Landwehr, M.D., and Mark Boguniewicz, M.D., "Current Perspectives on Latex Allergy," *Journal of Pediatrics*, vol. 128, no. 3, March 1996, pp. 305–312.

14. Allen P. Kaplan, M.D., Rebecca H. Buckley, M.D., and Kenneth P. Mathews, M.D., "Allergic Skin Disorders," *Journal of the American Medical Association*, vol. 258, no. 20, November 27, 1987, pp. 2900–2909.

15. "Contact Dermatitis and Uticaria from Environmental Exposures," *American Family Physician*, vol. 48, no. 5, October 1993, p. 773.

16. Sandra Fish, "People Suffering from Chemical Sensitivity Have Trouble Finding Help," *Daily Camera*, Knight-Ridder/Tribune News Service, February 16, 1996.

17. Thomas L. Kurt, M.D., M.P.H., "Multiple Chemical Sensitivities—A Syndrome of Pseudotoxicity Manifest as Exposure Perceived Symptoms," *A Journal of Toxicology: Clinical Toxicology*, vol. 33, no. 2, 1995, pp. 101–105.

18. American Academy of Allergy, Asthma and Immunology, "Position Statement on Candidiasis Hypersensitivity Syndrome," *Journal of Allergy and Clinical Immunology*, vol. 78, no. 2, August 1986, pp. 271–272.

Chapter 4. Diagnosing Allergies

1. Erika and Kevin Weiberg, interview with the author, October 10, 1996.

2. William J. Davis, "Evaluating Allergies," in *The Columbia University College of Physicians & Surgeons Complete Home Medical Guide*, revised edition, ed. Donald F. Tapley, M.D., Thomas Q. Morris, M.D., Lewis P. Rowland, M.D., and Robert J. Weiss, M.D. (New York: Crown Publishers, Inc., 1989), p. 679.

3. Stuart H. Young, M.D., Bruce Dobozin, M.D., and Margaret Miner, *Allergies: The Complete Guide to Diagnosis, Treatment, and Daily Management* (Yonkers, N.Y.: Consumer Reports Books, 1991), p. 22.

4. "AAAAI Position Statement 8: Controversial Techniques," *Journal of Allergy and Clinical Immunology*, vol. 67, no. 5, May 1981, pp. 336–337.

5. National Heart, Lung and Blood Institute's National Asthma Education and Prevention Program, Expert Panel Report 2: "Guidelines for the Diagnosis and Management of Asthma," February 1997, pp. 1a–10. This report may be downloaded from the Internet at http://www.nhlbi.nih.gov/nhlbi/lung/asthma/prof/asthgdln.htm

6. Allen P. Kaplan, M.D., Rebecca H. Buckley, M.D., and Kenneth P. Mathews, M.D., "Allergic Skin Disorders," *Journal of the American Medical Association*, vol. 258, no. 20, November 27, 1987, pp. 2900–2909.

7. Hugh A. Sampson, M.D., and Dean D. Metcalfe, M.D., "Food Allergies," *Journal of the American Medical Association*, vol. 268, no. 20, November 25, 1992, p. 2843.

8. Joanne Silberner, "Allergy Warfare," *U.S. News & World Report*, February 20, 1989, p. 69.

Chapter 5. Preventing Allergies

1. Kathy M. Kristof, "Allergies Pose Challenge for Clinton Health Plan," *Los Angeles Times*, October 24, 1993, p. D4.

2. Andrew M. Pope, Ph.D., "Indoor Allergens—Assessing and Controlling Adverse Health Effects," *Journal of the American Medical Association*, vol. 269, no. 21, June 2, 1993, p. 2721.

3. Joanne Silberner, "Allergy Warfare," *U.S. News and World Report*, February 20, 1989, pp. 69–77.

4. Stuart H. Young, M.D., Bruce S. Dobozin, M.D., and Margaret Miner, *Allergies: The Complete Guide to Diagnosis, Treatment, and Management* (Yonkers, N.Y.: Consumer Reports Books, 1991), p. 140.

5. William J. Davis, "Allergic Rhinitis—Pollen," in *The Columbia University College of Physicians and Surgeons Complete Home Medical Guide*, revised edition, ed. Donald F. Tapley, M.D., Thomas Q. Morris, M.D., Lewis P. Rowland, M.D., and Robert J. Weiss, M.D. (New York: Crown Publishers, Inc., 1989), p. 683.

6. Susan Duerksen, "A Menace Uncovered," *The San Diego Union-Tribune*, April 15, 1996, p. A1.

7. Bob Condor, "Food Can Be Deadly to Allergic," *Chicago Tribune*, September 6, 1995 (Evening edition), sec. 2, p. 1.

8. Susan Carlton, "Living with Food Allergies," *Parents*, August 1995, pp. 28–31.

9. U. M. Saarinen and M. Kajosaari, "Breast-feeding as Prophylaxis Against Atopic Disease: Prospective Follow-up Study Until 17 Years Old," *Lancet*, vol. 346, October 21, 1995, pp. 1065–1069.

10. R. Sporik, S. T. Holgate, T. A. E. Platts-Mills, and J. J. Cogswell, "Exposure to House-dust Mite Allergen (*Der p* I) and the Development of Asthma in Childhood: A Prospective Study," *New England Journal of Medicine*, 1990, vol. 323, no. 8, August 23, 1990, pp. 502–507.

11. H. Arshad, "Pets and Atopic Disorders in Infancy," *British Journal of Clinical Practice*, 1991, vol. 45, pp. 88–89.

12. K. Barber, E. Mussin, and D. K. Taylor, "Fetal Exposure to Involuntary Maternal Smoking and Childhood Respiratory Disease," *Annals of Allergy, Asthma, and Immunology*, vol. 76, no. 5, May 1996, pp. 427–430.

13. T. Schäfer, P. Dirschedl, B. Kunz, J. Ring, and K. Uberla, "Maternal Smoking During Pregnancy and Lactation Increases the Risk for Atopic Eczema in the Offspring," *Journal of the American Academy of Dermatology*, vol. 36, no. 4, April 1997, pp. 550–556.

14. D. W. Hide, S. Matthews, S. Tariq, and S. H. Arshad, "Allergen Avoidance in Infancy and Allergy at 4 Years of Age," *Allergy*, vol. 51, no. 2, February 1996, pp. 89–93.

Chapter 6. Treating Allergies

1. DeWitt, interview with the author, November 7, 1996.

2. Robin Marantz Henig, "Asthma Kills," *The New York Times Magazine*, March 28, 1993, p. 50.

3. Robert Berkow, M.D., editor-in-chief, *The Merck Manual of Diagnosis and Therapy* (Rahway, N.J.: Merck & Co., Inc., 1987), pp. 630–631.

4. Allen P. Kaplan, M.D., Rebecca H. Buckley, M.D., and Kenneth P. Mathews, M.D., "Allergic Skin Disorders," *Journal of the American Medical Association*, vol. 258, no. 20, November 27, 1987, p. 2902.

5. Stephen F. Kemp, M.D., and Richard F. Lockey, M.D., "Peanut Anaphylaxis from Food Cross-Contamination," *Journal of the American Medical Association,* June 5, 1996, pp. 1636–1637.

6. Martin D. Valentine, M.D., "Anaphylaxis and Stinging Insect Hypersensitivity," *Journal of the American Medical Association,* vol. 268, no. 20, November 25, 1992, pp. 2831–2832.

7. Peter S. Creticos, M.D., "Immunotherapy with Allergens," *Journal of the American Medical Association,* vol. 268, no. 20, November 25, 1992, pp. 2834–2839.

8. Susan Weiberg, interview with the author, December 4, 1996.

9. Creticos, pp. 2834–2839.

10. Isadora B. Stehlin, "Taking a Shot at Allergy Relief," *FDA Consumer,* May 1996, pp. 7–11.

11. A. J. Frew, "Injection Immunotherapy," *British Medical Journal,* vol. 307, no. 6909, October 9, 1993, pp. 919–923.

Chapter 7. The High Cost of Allergies

1. Robin Marantz Henig, "Asthma Kills," *The New York Times Magazine,* March 28, 1993, p. 42.

2. Centers for Disease Control, "Asthma Mortality and Hospitalization Among Children and Young Adults—United States, 1980–1993," *Morbidity and Mortality Weekly Report,* vol. 45, no. 17, May 3, 1996, pp. 350–353.

3. American College of Allergy, Asthma and Immunology, "Rising Asthma Deaths 'Inexcusable,' According to Allergist Organization," *Allergy, Asthma, and Immunology Online,* May 23, 1996, <http://allergy.mcg.edu/news/n5.html> (January 14, 1998).

4. Hoechst Marion Roussel, "New Survey Takes a Look into Daily Lives of Allergy Sufferers," *Doctor's Guide to Medical and Other News*, August 20, 1996, <http://www.pslgroup.com/dg/9f4a.htm> (January 14, 1998).

5. Richard M. Schulz, Ph.D., Joseph Dye, B.S., Lynn Jolicoeur, Pharm.D., Thomas Cafferty, Ph.D., and Jan Watson, M.S., "Quality-of-Life Factors for Parents of Children with Asthma," *Journal of Asthma*, vol. 31, no. 3, 1994, pp. 209–219.

6. Michael Kaliner, M.D., and Robert Lemanske, M.D., "Rhinitis and Asthma," *Journal of the American Medical Association*, vol. 268, no. 20, November 25, 1992, p. 2828.

7. Sherry Helms, "Fighting Allergies: What Really Works," *Consumers Digest*, vol. 35, no. 4, July–August 1996, p. 23.

8. Ellen Neuborne, "Allergy Season: No Relief for Employers," *USA Today*, April 8, 1996, p. B1.

9. Dori Stehlin, "Latex Allergies: When Rubber Rubs the Wrong Way," *FDA Consumer*, vol. 26, no. 7, September 1996, pp. 16–21.

10. Taro Shirakawa, Tadao Enomoto, Shin-ichiro Shumazu, and Julian M. Hopkin, "The Inverse Association Between Tuberculin Responses and Atopic Disorder," *Science*, vol. 275, January 3, 1997, pp. 77–79.

11. American College of Allergy, Asthma and Immunology.

Chapter 8. The Future of Allergy Research

1. Naomi Freundlich, "No More Sneezing, Itching, Coughing? Science Is Working to Prevent Allergic Reactions," *Business Week*, October 16, 1995, pp. 76–78.

2. J. M. McDonnell, A. J. Beavil, G. A. Mackay, B. A. Jameson, R. Korngold, H. J. Gould, and B. J. Sutton, "Structure-based Design and Characterization of Peptides That Inhibit IgE Binding to Its High-affinity Receptor," *Nature Structural Biology*, vol. 3, no. 5, May 1996, pp. 419–425.

3. J. E. de Vries and H. Yssel, "Modulation of the Human IgE Response," *European Respiratory Journal*, 1996, vol. 9, suppl. 22, pp. 58s–62s.

4. Philip S. Norman, John L. Ohman, Jr., A. A. Long, Peter S. Creticos, Malcolm A. Gefter, Ze'ev Shaked, Robert A. Wood, Peyton A. Eggleston, Kerry B. Hafner, Patricia Rao, Lawrence M. Lichtenstein, N. H. Jones, and Christopher F. Nicodemus, "Treatment of Cat Allergy with T-cell Reactive Peptides," *American Journal of Respiratory and Critical Care Medicine*, vol. 154, 1996, pp. 1623–1628.

5. Freundlich, pp. 76–78.

6. Ching-Hsiang Hsu, Kaw-Yan Chua, Mi-Hua Tao, Yih-Loong Lai, Heuy-Dong Wu, Shau-Ku Huang, and Kue-Hsiung Hsieh, "Immunoprophylaxis of Allergen-Induced Immunoglobulin E Synthesis and Airway Hyper-responsiveness *in vivo* by Genetic Immunization," *Nature Medicine*, vol. 2, no. 5, May 1996, pp. 540–544.

7. Hugh Sampson, interview with the author, December 12, 1996.

8. Taro Shirakawa, Airong Li, Michael Dubowitz, James W. Dekker, Ann E. Shaw, Jennie A. Faux, Chisei Ra, William O.C.M. Cookson, and Julian M. Hopkin, "Association Between Atopy and Variants of the ß Subunit of the High-affinity Immunoglobulin E Receptor," *Nature Genetics*, vol. 7, June 1994, pp. 125–130.

9. "How Mothers Pass On Asthma," *New Scientist,* June 11, 1994, p. 18.

10. David G. Marsh, John D. Neely, Daniel R. Breazeale, Balaram Ghosh, Linda R. Friedhoff, Eva Erlich-Kautzky, Carsten Schou, Guha Krishnaswamy, and Terri H. Beaty, "Linkage Analysis of IL4 and Other Chromosome 5q31.1 Markers and Total Serum Immunoglobulin E Concentrations," *Science,* vol. 264, May 20, 1994, pp. 1152–1156.

11. Susan M. MacDonald, Thorunn Rafner, Jacqueline Langdon, Lawrence M. Lichtenstein, "Molecular Identification of an IgE-Dependent Histamine-Releasing Factor," *Science,* vol. 269, August 4, 1995, pp. 688–690.

Glossary

allergen—Any substance, such as pollen or certain foods, capable of provoking an allergic reaction. Allergens may enter through the body through the respiratory system, the digestive system, the eyes, or through contact with the skin.

allergen immunotherapy—Also called allergy shots or desensitization therapy, immunotherapy involves giving gradually increasing doses of the purified allergen extracts. It causes the immune system to become less sensitive to certain allergens. Allergen immunotherapy is an effective treatment for allergies to insect venom; tree, grass, or weed pollens; and, to a lesser extent, dust mites, mold, and cat dander.

allergic rhinitis—An inflammation of the mucous membrane of the nose. Plant pollens and outdoor molds cause seasonal allergic rhinitis; house dust mites, indoor molds, or animal dander cause perennial allergic rhinitis.

allergy—Abnormal reactivity of the immune system to normally harmless substances.

anaphylaxis—A severe, potentially life-threatening allergic reaction that takes place throughout the body.

antibody—Also called an immunoglobulin, an antibody is a protein made by B cells (a type of white blood cell). Antibodies have specialized combining sites that react specifically with foreign substances.

antigen—Any substance that can trigger an immune response. Many antigens are foreign proteins carried on the surfaces of bacteria, viruses, and other disease-causing organisms. Allergens are a special type of antigen, capable of causing an allergic reaction.

antihistamines—Drugs that block the effects of histamine (*see* histamine).

antitoxin—An antibody that combines with a toxin, neutralizing its toxicity.

asthma—A breathing disorder, often triggered by allergies, characterized by tightness of the chest and labored breathing, along with coughing, gasping, and wheezing.

atopic dermatitis—An inflammation of the skin, usually accompanied by patches of dry, itchy, scaly skin. Also known as eczema, atopic dermatitis is often triggered by food and environmental allergens.

B cell—A lymphocyte capable of producing antibodies.

basophil—A white blood cell that stores histamine and has IgE receptors on its surface. The basophil circulates in the blood, releasing potent chemicals involved in both the immediate and the late-phase allergic response.

bronchodilators—Drugs that widen the bronchi, or airways. Bronchodilators are commonly used in the treatment of asthma.

bronchus—Any of the larger airways that connect the trachea (windpipe) to the lungs. The plural form of "bronchus" is "bronchi."

chronic—Prolonged or lingering. Many allergic diseases, such as asthma, are chronic; they can be controlled, but not cured.

contact dermatitis—An inflammation or rash of the skin, caused by contact with various chemical, animal, or plant substances. The reaction may be caused by a T cell-mediated allergic reaction (*see* delayed-type hypersensitivity) or by direct toxic effect of the substance. Nickel, latex, cosmetics, and certain plants such as poison ivy are all common causes of contact dermatitis.

corticosteroid drugs—An anti-inflammatory group of drugs similar to the corticosteroid hormones produced in the body. They are often used to treat asthma, allergic rhinitis, contact dermatitis, and eczema.

delayed-type hypersensitivity—A T cell-mediated allergic reaction that develops twenty-four to forty-eight hours after exposure to an antigen. Allergic contact dermatitis is a delayed-type hypersensitivity reaction.

digestive system—A group of organs, including the stomach, the large and small intestines, and the colon, that break down foods into their chemical components. Food allergies often take place in the digestive system.

DNA—Deoxyribonucleic acid. DNA, the major molecule in cell chromosomes, plays a central role in determining inherited traits.

eczema—*See* atopic dermatitis.

epinephrine—A naturally occurring hormone, also called adrenaline. Synthetic epinephrine is the drug of choice for treating anaphylaxis and sometimes severe asthma attacks. It increases the heart rate, dilates the airways to improve breathing, and narrows blood vessels.

gene—A unit of heredity composed of DNA. Each gene is located on a specific site of the chromosome and determines some characteristic such as eye color. Each individual carries two copies of every gene, one inherited from each parent.

hay fever—*See* allergic rhinitis.

histamine—A chemical present in cells throughout the body, especially mast cells and basophils. Released during an allergic reaction, histamine is one of the chemicals responsible for inflammation, and is the major reason for the runny nose, sneezing, and itching in allergic rhinitis. Histamine also narrows the bronchi in asthma attacks.

hives—A skin condition, also known as urticaria, characterized by itchy raised white lumps surrounded by an area of red inflammation. Hives may be triggered by a number of food, drug, or respiratory allergens.

IgE—The antibody type involved in allergic reactions and parasitic infections.

immediate hypersensitivity—An allergic reaction, either local or throughout the body, mediated by the interaction between antigen (allergen) and IgE antibodies carried on the surfaces of mast cells and basophils.

immune system—A group of organs, cells, and molecules that protect the body against foreign substances.

immunoglobulin—*See* antibody.

inflammation—Redness, swelling, heat, and pain, accompanied by an infiltration of white blood cells in a tissue. Inflammation can be caused by an infection or by chemical or physical injury. Allergic reactions often cause inflammation.

interleukins—A group of chemicals, produced by lymphocytes or monocytes, that regulate the immune response. Interleukin 4 (IL4), produced by T helper 2 (TH2) cells, stimulates B cells to produce IgE antibodies.

lymphocytes—White blood cells critical to the immune system's specific adaptive responses to foreign substances. B cells and T cells are both lymphocytes.

mast cell—A white blood cell that stores histamine and has IgE receptors on its surface. The mast cell, generally found on the epithelium (the layer of cells covering surfaces that make contact with the outside world) and connective tissue, releases potent chemicals involved in both the immediate and the late-phase allergic response.

phagocytes—White blood cells that engulf and destroy foreign substances. Some, most notably the macrophages, present antigen to T cells and produce chemical messengers that regulate the immune system.

placebo—An inactive substance given as a control, or comparison, in an experiment or test.

RAST—An abbreviation for radioallergosorbent test, a trademark of Pharmacia Diagnostics. RAST is a laboratory test to detect IgE antibodies to specific allergens.

receptors—Molecules on the outside or inside of a cell membrane that specifically bind to a particular chemical group.

respiratory system—The group of organs responsible for carrying oxygen from the air to the bloodstream, and for getting rid of carbon dioxide. Allergic rhinitis and asthma take place in the respiratory system.

serum—The clear, yellowish fluid that remains after suspended material (such as blood cells and other solid particles) are removed from the blood. The serum contains, among other things, antibodies.

skin test—An allergy test in which a small amount of allergen is lightly scratched into, or sometimes injected just under, the skin.

systemic—Affecting the body generally; not local.

T cell—Lymphocytes that regulate the immune response, kill cancer cells or virus-infected cells, or mediate delayed-type hypersensitivity reactions. Helper T cells stimulate B cells to produce antibodies, or cooperate with other T cells in regulating the immune system. One subset of T helper cell, TH2, is responsible for turning on B cell production of IgE.

vaccine—A preparation containing disease-causing microbes or toxins, rendered harmless in the laboratory, and administered to people or animals, to induce the development of immunity against that organism. Vaccination is also known as immunization.

Further Reading

Books

"Allergies." Chapter 20 in *Mayo Clinic Family Health Book.* David E. Larson, M.D., Editor-in-Chief. New York, N.Y.: William Morrow and Co., Inc., 1990.

Bierman, C. Warren, M.D., and David S. Pearlman, M.D., eds. *Allergic Diseases from Infancy to Adulthood.* 2nd edition. Philadelphia, Pa.: W. B. Saunders Company, 1988.

Brookes, Tim. *Catching My Breath: An Asthmatic Explores His Illness.* New York: Vintage Books, 1995.

Edelson, Edward. *Allergies: The Encyclopedia of Health: Medical Disorders and Their Treatment.* New York: Chelsea House Publishers, 1989.

Middleton, Elliott Jr., M.D., Charles E. Reed, M.D., Elliot F. Ellis, M.D., N. Franklin Adkinson, Jr., M.D., John W. I. Yunginger, M.D., and William W. Busse, M.D., eds. *Allergy: Principles and Practice.* 4th edition (2 volumes). St. Louis, Mo.: Mosby Year-Book, Inc., 1993.

Silverstein, Alvin and Virginia, and Laura Silverstein Nunn. *Asthma.* Springfield, N.J.: Enslow Publishers, Inc., 1997.

Silverstein, Arthur M. *A History of Immunology.* San Diego, Calif.: Academic Press, 1989.

Young , Stuart H., M.D., Bruce S. Dobozin, M.D., Margaret Miner, and the editors of Consumer Reports Books. *Allergies: The Complete Guide to Diagnosis, Treatment, and Daily Management.* Yonkers, N.Y.: Consumer Reports Books, 1991.

Articles

Anderson, John A., M.D. "Allergic Reactions to Drugs and Biological Agents." *Journal of the American Medical Association,* vol. 268, no. 20, November 25, 1992, pp. 2845–2857.

Brown, Abe. "All About Allergy and Asthma." *Current Health 2,* October 1993, pp. 6–11.

Creticos, Peter S., M.D. "Immunotherapy with Allergens." *Journal of the American Medical Association,* vol. 268, no. 20, November 25, 1992, pp. 2834–2839.

Helms, Sherry. "Fighting Allergies: What Really Works." *Consumer's Digest,* vol. 35, no. 4, July–August 1996, p. 23.

Henig, Robin Marantz. "Asthma Kills." *New York Times Magazine,* March 28, 1993, p. 42.

Hingley, Audrey T. "Food Allergies: When Eating Is Risky." *FDA Consumer,* December 1993, pp. 27–31.

Kaliner, Michael, M.D., and Robert Lemanske, M.D. "Rhinitis and Asthma." *Journal of the American Medical Association,* vol. 268, no. 20, November 25, 1992, pp. 2807–2829.

Kaplan, Allen P., M.D., Rebecca H. Buckley, M.D., and Kenneth P. Mathews, M.D. "Allergic Skin Disorders." *Journal of the American Medical Association,* vol. 268, no. 20, November 25, 1992, pp. 2900–2909.

Katzenstein, Larry. "Allergies: Nothing to Sneeze At." *American Health*, May 1993, p. 44.

Lichtenstein, Lawrence M. "Allergy and the Immune System." *Scientific American*, September 1993, pp. 85–93.

Radetsky, Peter. "Of Parasites and Pollen." *Discover*, September 1993, pp. 54–62.

Rosenthal, Elizabeth. "Burning Down the House." *Discover*, May 1993, pp. 30–32.

Sampson, Hugh A., M.D., and Dean D. Metcalfe, M.D. "Food Allergies." *Journal of the American Medical Association*, vol. 268, no. 20, November 25, 1992, pp. 2840–2844.

Seligson, Susan V. "The Big Sneeze." *Health*, September 1995, p. 92.

Stehlin, Dori. "Latex Allergies: When Rubber Rubs the Wrong Way." *FDA Consumer*, September 1996, pp. 16–21.

Stehlin, Isadora B. "Taking a Shot at Allergy Relief." *FDA Consumer*, May 1996, pp. 7–11.

Valentine, Martin D., M.D. "Anaphylaxis and Stinging Insect Hypersensitivity." *Journal of the American Medical Association*, vol. 268, no. 20, November 25, 1992, pp. 2830–2833.

Index

latex allergies, 12, 37, 39, 44–46, 68, 88
Lucretius, 14
lymphocytes, 24

M

MacDonald, Susan, 97–98
macrophage, 27–28, 30, 31
Marsh, David, 96-97
mast cell, 31–33, 34, 35, 37, 39, 42, 46, 75, 83, 91, 92, 96, 97
milk, 26, 42, 43, 59, 70, 71
mold, 26, 35–36, 37, 53, 60, 61, 62, 64
multiple chemical sensitivity, 48–49

N

New England Medical Center, 94
nickel, 12, 24, 26, 48
Noon, Leonard, 24
Novardis, 91

O

Ottesen, Eric, 34

P

parasites, 30, 34
Pasteur, Louis, 17
peanuts, 13, 42, 70, 71, 79–80, 95–96
penicillin, 12, 13, 43–44, 56
pets, 26, 36, 48, 53, 54, 60, 61–62, 73, 90, 94
phagocytes, 27, 48,
poison ivy, 12, 24, 48, 67, 78
pollen, 12, 15, 17, 24, 26, 30–31, 35, 36, 37, 38, 46, 53, 61, 63, 65, 82, 90, 94
Portier, Paul, 17–18, 24
Portuguese man-of-war, 17–18
Prausnitz, Carl, 20–21, 22
psychological factors, 37, 46, 47, 49, 85, 87

R

radioallergosorbent test (RAST), 59

ragweed, 35, 38, 55, 64, 67, 94
rash, 13, 19, 26, 42, 43, 47, 48, 51, 52, 58, 79, 85, 87
Richet, Charles, 17–18, 24
Rinkel method, 55
Rosenau, Milton, 20

S

Sampson, Hugh, 96
Schick, Béla, 20
sea anemone, 18
Selner, John, 13
sensitization, 31, 32
serum sickness, 20
skin allergies, 24, 46–48
skin patch test, 56, 58
skin prick test, 56, 59
skin test, 58, 59
soy products, 42–43, 70, 71

T

T cells, 24, 28, 30, 31, 33, 48, 83, 93–94, 95, 96
Tanox, 91
theophylline, 77
tobacco smoke, 63, 71, 89
tuberculin, 21–22
tuberculosis, 21–22, 48, 88

U

uticaria. *See* hives.

V

vaccines, 17–18, 94–96
Van Dyken, Amy, 9, 10, 12
von Behring, Emil, 18–19
von Pirquet, 20, 22

W

wasps, 14, 41, 66
wheat, 42, 70, 71
work-related allergies, 87–88

Y

yellow jackets, 41, 66